MAJOR GRANVILLE HALLER
Dismissed with Malice

Guy Breshears

HERITAGE BOOKS
2006

HERITAGE BOOKS

AN IMPRINT OF HERITAGE BOOKS, INC.

Books, CDs, and more—Worldwide

For our listing of thousands of titles see our website at
www.HeritageBooks.com

Published 2006 by
HERITAGE BOOKS, INC.
Publishing Division
65 East Main Street
Westminster, Maryland 21157-5026

Copyright © 2006 Guy Breshears
Cover photograph of Col. Granville Haller courtesy of
University of Washington Libraries, Special Collections, UW2961

Other Books by the Author:
Loyal till Death: A Diary of the 13th New York Artillery

All rights reserved. No part of this book may be reproduced or transmitted in any form or by any means, electronic or mechanical, including photocopying, recording or by any information storage and retrieval system without written permission from the author, except for the inclusion of brief quotations in a review.

International Standard Book Number: **0-7884-3801-8**

TABLE OF CONTENTS

PREFACE	v
FOREWORD	vii
DISMISSAL OF MAJOR HALLER	1
REACTION TO DISMISSAL	1
IN DEFENSE OF MAJOR HALLER	21
CIVIL WAR EVENTS	41
CONGRESSIONAL ACTION	69
PROCEEDINGS OF THE COURT OF INQUIRY	
FIRST DAY	77
SECOND DAY	79
THIRD DAY	79
FOURTH DAY	86
FIFTH DAY	94
SIXTH DAY	104
SEVENTH DAY	107
FINDINGS AND OPINIONS OF THE COURT	115
OPINIONS TO THE COURT OF INQUIRY	119
AFTER THE COURT OF INQUIRY	135
COURT EXHIBIT A	141
COURT EXHIBIT B	143
DEPOSITION OF GEN. ROBERT C. SCHENCK	145
COURT EXHIBIT F	147
DEPOSITION OF CLARK H. WELLS	149
BIBLIOGRAPHY	153
INDEX	155
ABOUT THE AUTHOR	159

Introduction

Major Granville Owen Haller, Seventh Infantry Regiment, United States Army was dismissed from military service without facing his accuser; he neither had a trial nor was he even notified that he faced any type of indictment.

Who was Major Haller? In the annals of US history he generally doesn't even rate a footnote. He was an unassuming officer, like many others who served, who did his best to carry out the duties assigned to him. Even in Washington State history he barely gets mentioned, or is even remembered, even though his military investigation into the death of an Indian sub-agent plunged the Northwest into three years of warfare against the various Indian tribes that lived there. He is also barely remembered for his return to the Puget Sound region many years later, when he became one of the state's prominent citizens.

He served his country honorably and faithfully. Directly commissioned as an officer, he first saw combat in the Second Seminole Indian war in Florida. Then, during the war against Mexico, he was brevetted twice for gallantry, at the battles of Molino Del Rey and Chapultepec. Later he served against various Indian groups in the Pacific Northwest, participated in the dispute over the ownership of the San Juan Islands, and finally he saw duty in the Civil War, when he was dismissed.

Who was Haller's accuser? Lieutenant Clark H. Wells, US Navy, and very little is known about him. What caused him to write a letter about Haller, and to whom did he write it? Was Wells a supporter of the anti-General McClellan group, and since he felt slighted by Haller he knew where to get his revenge? If he felt slighted, why didn't he ask the Masonic Order to try his fellow Mason? Finally, did Wells know that his letter would bring the downfall of Haller?

As for the War Department, one can only speculate what caused them to proceed to dismiss Haller. Perhaps it was because Secretary of War Edwin Stanton and Judge Advocate General Joseph Holt hated McClellan and sought to undermine him, which could include going after those who supported McClellan. One can only wonder if there was a conspiracy to undermine McClellan's support, and how many officers were dismissed or denied promotions and commands because of their support.

President Lincoln spoke to Congress on December 1, 1862:

"Fellow-citizens, we cannot escape history. We of this Congress and this administration, will be remembered in spite of ourselves. No personal significance, or insignificance, can spare one or another of us. The fiery trial through which we pass, will light us down, in honor or dishonor, to the latest generation."

Now is the time to remember and honor a man who served his country well and yet whose country decided to dismiss him at a time when the United States needed men to preserve the Union. It is now time to pass judgment on Lincoln's Administration for what they have done and what they have failed to do.

I would like to thank the staffs at the National Archives and Records Administration, United States Army Military History Institute, Pennsylvania House Archives and Records Center, Island County (Washington) Historical Society, Fort Dalles (Oregon) Museum/Anderson Homestead. Also, Dr. JWT Youngs, Jim Tyrrell, and everyone at Heritage Books, Inc., especially my editor Roxanne Carlson.

This book is dedicated to those who served with honor in the United States Military: past, present and future.

Finally, to my mother who will be there when I have to face my own judgment. May I be found to have served faithfully and with honor.

I saw under the sun in the place of judgment wickedness, and in the place of justice iniquity. —Ecclesiastes 3:16

Foreword

Guy Breshears' book is the result of years of painstaking detailed historic research. Far from being a boring esoteric academic exercise, the author's work serves to introduce readers to one of the most interesting men of the mid- to late 1800s. He provides the reader with an insight into the life of a courageous and able career military officer, victim of a grossly unfair dismissal from military service, and successful businessman of the era.

Few people who walk pass the headstones in Lot 496 of Seattle's Lake View Cemetery take the time to notice, or if they do notice, are aware of the significance of the name Colonel Granville Owen Haller on one of the monuments. The unfortunate factor in this scenario is that the people who do not notice or recognize Granville Haller's name are missing out on an opportunity to pay their respects to a man who made significant contributions to the development of the nation and more particularly the Puget Sound Region.

Although generally ignored by today's historians, Colonel Haller played a part in many of the significant events that occurred during his lifetime. He associated with some of the most prominent people of his time. He also was the patriarch of one of the most socially and financially prominent families in the Puget Sound region. Those who have taken the time to research Colonel Haller's life find him to be a truly amazing character. To put it in clear contemporary language, Granville Haller was a standup guy whose life could have, or should have served as the basis for historic recognition, historic novels and/or action movies.

Granville Haller was born in 1819 and raised by his widowed mother in York, Pennsylvania with an older brother and younger sister. Ignoring his mother's objections, he unsuccessfully pursued an appointment to West Point. In 1839, at the age of twenty, after being denied an appointment to West Point, he succeeded in obtaining a direct commission as a second lieutenant.

As a second lieutenant, he participated in the Second Seminole War and was involved in the firefight in which Captain John Dade was killed. He participated in the action that resulted in the capture of one of the leaders of the Second Seminole uprising. As a first lieutenant, he served in the Mexican War under General Zachary Taylor and received brevet promotions to captain, and then to major, for gallantry and meritorious conduct. His courage as a soldier and ability as a military officer was mentioned in dispatches along with the names of then Captains Ulysses S. Grant and Phillip Sheridan.

In 1853, as a brevet major he brought his wife and young children around the Cape to his assignment at Fort Dalles near the Columbia River. At the time, Fort Dalles was an isolated post in the Oregon Territory. The fort was used as a base for military patrols along the Oregon Trail. Haller and his troops protected the settlers in the expanding territory and occasionally escorted immigrant wagon trains. While assigned to Fort Dalles, he led two punitive expeditions against a group of Indians responsible for the brutal torture and murder of twenty immigrants—men, women, and children—during the so-called "Ward Massacre." During these two expeditions Major Haller captured several of the offenders, brought them back to the site of the massacre, and had them hanged over the graves of the massacre victims.

In 1855, upon his return from his second punitive expedition to avenge the Ward Massacre victims, he was assigned to lead a group of about 120 soldiers and support personnel into hostile Yakima Indian Territory. This was done both as a show of force and to investigate the disappearance and suspected murder of an Indian agent. This effort did not go well. Haller was initially confronted and attacked by a combined force of about 700 Yakima, Klickitat, Cayuse and other Indians. This initial opposing Indian force of about 700 quickly grew to an estimated 1,500 by the second day of the running battle. This battle, known at the time as "Haller's Defeat," is generally viewed as the start of the Indian Wars in Washington State.

In 1856, Haller was assigned to build Fort Townsend and run boat patrols around Puget Sound to protect settlers and peaceful Puget Sound Indians from the hostile Indians coming down from Canada and Alaska. During one boat patrol Haller and his troops captured a group of Nooksack Indians that was about to attack Fort Whatcom (now Bellingham, Washington). Haller presented his captives to Captain George Pickett, the Fort Whatcom commander, as hostages to be held as insurance against further attacks by the Nooksacks.

In 1859, during the international boundary dispute concerning the San Juan Islands, also called the "Pig War," Major Haller landed with reinforcements on the Islands in an attempt to stabilize a potential for armed confrontation between American soldiers under Captain Pickett and British forces. Haller was relieved by General Harney and briefly reassigned to Fort Vancouver, Washington.

In 1860, after his brief stay at Fort Vancouver, he was assigned to Fort Mojave, New Mexico. When the Civil War started, Major Haller was reassigned as the Provost Marshall for Maryland and Virginia and commanded the Headquarters Guard for General McClellan's Army of the Potomac. During the Battle of Gettysburg, he was placed in command of the local militia and led 350 citizen soldiers in futile efforts to delay Confederate General Jubal Early's six-thousand-man force as it entered the York, Pennsylvania area. In July 1863, Haller was "dismissed" from the Army without a hearing or court martial, for allegedly making a disloyal statement at a drinking party in his tent. This adverse action was based entirely on the word of one Naval officer with a history of mental illness.

After his dismissal, Haller, his pregnant wife and four children, returned to Port Townsend, Washington, where he started farming, opened a store, and took over the Meigs boatyard and sawmill. The boatyard and sawmill failed. Haller succeeded as a storekeeper and was known to have granted credit to many pioneer settlers. Haller opened a second store and a warehouse in Coupeville, Washington, on Whidbey Island and continued granting credit to his customers, sometimes to financially dangerous levels. Over time, when the debtors gave up on homesteading, they would abandon their land claims and/or they would turn the land over to Haller as payment for their debts. During the period 1870 to 1871 Haller served as the Coupeville postmaster and Island County treasurer.

By the late 1870s, Haller had amassed land holdings in eleven counties, established several model farms, and became socially and financially prominent in the Puget Sound area—all this while working out of his Coupeville storefront. By 1879, Haller had enough wealth, power, and influence to have several politicians assist him in having his dismissal overturned. On March 3, 1879 Congress passed a resolution directing a re-evaluation of Haller's dismissal. As a result of the re-evaluation—sixteen years after his dismissal, at the age of fifty-nine—Granville Haller was reinstated in the military by joint resolution of Congress, as a colonel (the rank he would have reasonably achieved had he not been dismissed). As a result of his reinstatement in the Army, Granville and his wife left their relatively luxurious lifestyle for spartan military outposts.

After passing the Army's mandatory retirement age of sixty-three, and after spending about three years assigned to remote, if not desolate, forts in the Oklahoma Indian Territory; Haller retired to his three-story, eighteen-room mansion in Seattle's upscale First Hill neighborhood with the city's other socially and financially prominent families, including the Hanfords, the Burkes, the Rankes, the Collins, the Minors, the Stimsons, the Stacy's, the Blethens, and the Carkeeks.

Although retired from the military, Haller did not retire from life. With his sons, attorneys G. Morris Haller and Theodore N. Haller, his son G. Morris's law partner Thomas Burke, and others, Granville Haller continued to expand and develop his business interests. He platted the towns of Edison, Washington; Haller City (now part of Arlington), Washington; numerous sections of the City of Seattle; and other areas of the state.

He served as commander of the Seattle Home Guard -- a hastily established militia that protected the Chinese from hostile Seattleites during the 1886 Anti-Chinese Riots. He help established the Port Townsend's Masonic Lodge #6, served as the Masons' Grand Master of the Washington Territory, and remained an active Mason until his death. Granville Haller was a charter and life member of the Aztec Club, an organization of officers who fought in the Mexican War. Membership included almost all of the leaders – both sides – of the Civil War military. He was also active in several other military and fraternal organizations such as the Military Order of Foreign Wars, Loyal Legion, Order of Odd Fellows Pacific Lodge #63, and Washington Pioneer Society.

In 1897, at the age of seventy-eight, Colonel Granville O. Haller died in his home. The cause of his death is listed as "le Gripe." At the time of his death, Granville Haller and his wife Henrietta owned over 4,100 acres of farm and timber land; many additional acres, blocks, and lot of platted property; fractional interests in additional real property; stock in at least three banks; and other valuable assets.

Today many of the monuments to the Haller family are gone. The Haller Building, a five-story building constructed as one of the first brick structures built after the 1889 Seattle Fire, stood on the northwest corner of Second Avenue and Columbia Street and was razed in the 1950s. The Hallers' eighteen-room mansion called "Castlemont," built in 1883 at Minor Avenue and James Street, was razed in the 1940s. Haller City was annexed as part of the City of Arlington, Washington. Haller Street in West Seattle was renamed. The Haller School was relocated from SW 47th Avenue near Walker Street to Alaska Way and is now used as part of the West Seattle American Legion Hall.

However, if you pay attention and look carefully you can find remnants of the tributes to this man and his participation in the development of the region. The Haller fountains in Port Townsend and Bellingham; Haller Road on Whidbey Island; Haller Lake and the Haller Lake community in Seattle; Haller Streets in Edison, Arlington, and Prosser all bear witness to the contributions of this man who died in 1897.

Jim Tyrrell
Seattle, Washington

DISMISSAL OF MAJOR HALLER[1]

War Department
Adjutant General's Office
Washington, D.C., July 25th, 1863

Special Order No. 331 [extract]

By direction of the President, the following named officers are herby dismissed the service of the United States:
Major Granville O. Haller, 7th U.S. Infantry, for disloyal conduct and the utterance of disloyal sentiments.

By order of the Secretary of War,
E.D. Townsend,
Asst. Adj. General.

BACKGROUND AND REACTION

The accuser was Lt. Commander Clark H. Wells, U.S. Navy. It was on December 17, 1862, after the Union defeat at Fredericksburg that Haller invited several officers, including Wells, to his tent to share a bottle of alcohol. During the evening Haller asked Wells why he didn't cross a pontoon bridge, in Fredericksburg, in between Confederate artillery fire; Wells replied "Do you mean to say I was afraid?" Wells went on to insinuate that Haller was disloyal. He then further insulted him by asking if he could sleep in the tent of a Major Charles Whiting, 2nd US Calvary.
The next afternoon Wells came to Haller and begged of him not to tell anyone what had happened the previous night and that the matter was dropped. Haller was surprised when he heard from Wells in January 1863.

---

[1] No documentation has been found concerning the dismissal. Haller tried to obtain copies of any proceedings against him but all requests were returned with the words *The Secretary of War declines to accede to his request.* Speculation is that the Judge Advocate General of the Army, Col. Joseph Holt, hated Gen. George McClellan and that hatred was pointed towards the supporters, like Haller, of McClellan as well.

It should also be noted that Commander Wells, in 1861, spent 3 months in the Pennsylvania Hospital for the Insane at Philadelphia and was known to suffer from time to time[2].

York, PA
December 19, 1862

My Dear Major:

    I arrived home safely in a few hours after leaving General Franklin's[3] tent, and found all the folks well. Mrs. Haller and the children took supper with us last evening, and had you been present you would have enjoyed the oysters, which were very fine indeed. I enjoyed them the more, as my appetite had been sharpened by my *brief* campaign in Virginia.
    I gave your wife all the news, and when I had done, I found that I had not imparted anything that she had not seen in the papers. The people, as well as I can judge, are not dispirited in the least; those who sympathize with the South are exultant as a matter of course, and would no doubt give expression to their thoughts if they could do so with impunity[4].

---

[2] Lt. Commander Clark Henry Wells was born in 1822 at Reading, PA, appointed midshipman in 1840; attended the US Naval Academy in 1846 and became a passed midshipman that year. Saw action during the war with Mexico. Throughout the Civil War he served in a variety of commands including Commandant of the Philadelphia Navy Yard, early 1863; Commanded the *USS Galena*, late 1863 and participated in the Battle of Mobile Bay, August 1864; finished the war on duty at Hampton Roads. After the war commanded the *USS Kansas* in the South Atlantic, 1865-69. Promoted to commander, 1866 and captain 1871. Chief signal officer of the navy, 1879-80. Promoted to commodore, 1880 and commanded the Portsmouth Navy Yard; 1880-84. Promoted to rear-admiral in 1884 and retired that same year. Died in Washington, DC in 1888.
[3] General William Franklin, commanded the Left Grand Division, Army of the Potomac at this time
[4] Haller writes: Here he admits that he has not heard of a single instance where a person has given expression to his thoughts, but it is a matter of course, in his mind, that there are Southern sympathizers and they are exultant. Is not a clause like this mere slander?

All admire the gallant conduct of Franklin, inasmuch, that his friends here are going to present him with a sword, which is certainly deserving of, and which he will no doubt appreciate[5].

There is nothing else going on in town; even the battle of Saturday last is little talked of, which shows the phlegmatic character of our population.

I travelled to Washington in company of Lieut. B., (Corps of Engineers), and learned from him that you had another entertainment, the effects of which he felt in the shape of a headache. How do you stand it? I am afraid that these little social gatherings tend to make you express yourself too openly on political subjects, which some civilian might take advantage of, and use it to your prejudice, and so I would caution you to be more guarded[6].

I shall ever recollect my visit to the Army, and bear witness to the bravery and devotion of our troops. It has made a most pleasant impression upon my mind, and I am more confident than ever of our ultimate success.

Remember me kindly to Captain Cushing and to Major Whiting; also those whose names I cannot now recollect.

Lieut. Spaulding, 2d Cavalry, was kind enough to loan me his horse, when I rode to Franklin's Headquarters. I returned him the next day by an Orderly from Franklin's Corps. I hope he arrived safely, as he had been well taken care of.

Thank Mr. Spaulding for me for his horse and kind attention; also Dr. Wilson, who lives in the same tent with him.

I saw the Asst. Secretary of the Navy for a moment, and he assured me that I should be ordered as Captain of the Philadelphia Navy Yard; so I shall soon leave.

If I can be of any service to you let me know. I saw your brother this morning, and give him a brief account of yourself, and the military operations before Fredericksburg.

Look out for the bridge over the Potomac Creek, I came across in an open car, and, I felt very much like a man suspended by a wire. Let me hear from you soon.

---

[5] Haller writes: On my return to York, I found that the statement about the presentation of a sword was a mere freak of his imagination!

[6] Haller writes: Does not this imply that he would scorn, as all officers would, to take advantage of, and use to my prejudice, and opinions I express in the privacy of my tent to friends?

Sincerely yours,
C.H. Wells, U.S.N

Navy Yard, Philadelphia
January 16, 1863

Major Haller:

My dear sir: I should have replied to your letter before, but ever since my arrival at this station I have been kept very busy, and when night comes, I feel too tired to do anything but smoke and chat with the children; after all there is nothing like one's home, which you doubtless experienced for so many years.

Mrs. [name not recorded] is here on a visit for the purpose of procuring some little comforts for her brother, whom we saw. I am pleasantly situated, having for the first time in my naval career, a Government house to live in, but which I was obliged to furnish to some extent. Were it not that I have been away a year in the S.A.[South Atlantic] Squadron and for the sake of my family, I would prefer going to Sea in these exciting times, although my naval friends tell me that I have done my share; I think not, for I believe that no officer can do too much to assist in crushing out this sinful rebellion.

During my short visit to Gen. Franklin with whom I have been intimate for many years, I was glad to see that he was thoroughly Union in his sentiments, and had a horror of anything like disloyalty or secession. I have ever entertained a high opinion of his abilities as a man and as a solider. The sword will be presented to him will have inscribed upon it all the battles he has been engaged in[7]. I have heard from others in the camp that his bravery in the battle of Fredericksburg was of the highest order, and that alone entitles him to the distinguished honor of having a sword giving to him.

You mentioned in your letter that anything you may have said concerning the manner in which this war was carried on you would not hesitate to repeat[8]. At least I judge so. Do you recollect proposing the toast to Maj. Whiting? And which was the occasion of my leaving

---

[7] Haller writes: This was a most deliberate falsehood, for there was no sword.
[8] Haller writes: So far as my statements went, I would not hesitate to repeat them, but what he here says I uttered, my reader will see by Maj. Whiting's letter, is false in spirit as well as in letter.

your tent. "Here's to a Southern Confederacy, and a Northern one during the Administration of Lincoln," and another expression you had made use of before, in charging the President with loss of life in the battle of Fredericksburg, and that you believe "that I was the intention of the Administration to sacrifice the Army of the Potomac in the neighborhood of Richmond[9]. If these are your sentiments I would not hesitate to proclaim them, and were I to entertain such, I should resign my Commission. I do not mention these matters with a view of renewing any or causing unpleasant feeling, but merely to show you that you are doing yourself an injustice, for I cannot believe that you think so otherwise you would not remain in the Army. Were the opinions you have expressed before me and others made known, it would be exceedingly prejudicial to you. In these times it is the duty of all officers to sustain the Administration in the suppression of this rebellion. No mid-way course can be taken.

A year ago I was, what is termed a pro-slavery man, but I saw enough while down South to change my views entirely, for I regard Slavery as a curse to our Country, and the cause of this hell-born rebellion[10].

I believe there is nothing new in York; I have no affection for that place, as it contains a strong disloyal element, chiefly confined to those who have not shouldered the musket. If you should visit the city, I hope you will let me know. I regret very much to hear of the accident to Capt. Cushing but I hope ere this he has entirely recovered. This horseback riding I have always considered dangerous, I therefore never mounted a horse without feeling uncomfortable. Nothing like a ship after all.

That Galveston affair we all deplore, being the only mishap to our Navy since the breaking out of the rebellion. We lost four good officers by the premature blowing up of one of the Steamers[11]. The "Petapaco,"[12] a new Monitor was here two weeks ago. I regard her as invulnerable. She carries a gun weighing forty-one thousand pounds,

---

[9] Haller writes: This charge he voluntarily abandons in his letter to Secretary Stanton.

[10] When Wells wrote this he had bought and owned a slave that was currently in his service.

[11] On January 1, 1863 Confederate forces launched a successful attack to recapture the city of Galveston. 3 Union ships were captured and the *USS Westfield* by blown up by her crew to prevent capture.

[12] Most likely Wells is referring to the *USS Patapsco* commissioned in January, 1863.

and throws a ball of 450 lbs. Service, charge of 35 lbs., also two-hundred pound rifle. Altogether she is a most formidable vessel.

Kind regards to Maj. Whiting. Did Lieut. Spaulding of his regiment receive the horse which I had returned by one of Gen. Franklin's orderlies? Kind regards to Capt. Gibson and Franklin, should you meet with them. Let me hear from you, and believe me to be.

Yours sincerely,
C.H. Wells, U.S.N.

Navy Yard
Philadelphia, February 17th, 1863

Major Haller:

My dear sir: Since I wrote to you in reply to your letter, I have thought so much over what had occurred in your tent, and which was the cause of my leaving you, that I cannot see why I should not report your disloyal language to the Secretary of War, painful as it may be. But in these times when we are engaged in a deadly struggle to sustain our Government, I would sacrifice my son.

You uttered this expression in my presence, "Here's to a Northern Confederation and to a Southern one, while Lincoln is President," which you gave as a toast to Major Whiting in your tent, and had also said "that you considered the President responsible for the loss of life at the battle of Fredericksburg." No one can doubt my loyalty, and, I hope you will give me the credit if performing my duty conscientiously.[13]

---

[13] Haller writes: Now it has come to my knowledge and I can show by two witnesses, that his unfortunate man has spoken of an officer of the U.S. Navy, high in rank, as having a son who was at sea with the South Atlantic Squadron, and this son was in correspondence with the Rebel and was helping them, or words of similar import; and when he was asked why he had not reported the case to the Navy Department, the reply was: "It would only do me harm—it would bring down the Commodore on me," or words to that effect; show how "conscientiously" he has been performing his duty!

I am yours,
C.H. Wells,
Lieut. Commander, U.S.N.

Upon receiving the above letter Haller wrote the following to Wells.

York, Penna., February 18th, 1863

Lieut. Commander Clark H. Wells, U.S.N,
Commanding Navy Yard, Phila:

My dear sir: Your letter of the 16th of January and 17th of February, are received and contents noticed.
The absence of Major Whiting, U.S.A, on a Court Martial at the city of Washington, prevented my laying before him the former of the two letters, and getting from him a denial of the statements which you make, and then replying to yours. I shall not ask you to take my own statements. Fortunately, there was a witness present on the occasion of the conversation referred to in your letters, who saw all, heard all, and knows all that occurred[14].
I have not seen him since the receipt of your letters, and I think when called upon, he will remove the hallucination under which you seem to labor.
One thing I remember, and can hardly think that you have forgotten it. I gave a toast, and only one, it was:
"THE CONSTITUTION AS IT IS: THE UNION AS IT WAS!"
If this is disloyalty, then as Patrick Henry says: "Make the most of it!"
In the frame of mind in which you have written, it is obvious that all previous relations, however agreeable, are ignored. I shall not trouble you, therefore, with an account of your friends, or the on dits[15] of this place.

---

[14] This was Maj. Whiting whom Haller wanted to write to in order to put to rest the charges made by Wells. However, since Whiting was on court martial duty he was unavailable to responsed until released from this duty; therefore, Haller waited until Whiting's duty was finished.

[15] Definition: They say, or it is said. -- n. A flying report; rumor; as, it is a mere on dit; taken from the French meaning "they say"

As a Mason it is my duty to respect you as a brother, but I trust you will so conduct your course towards all brethren, that discord may not be charged upon you.

Fraternally yours,
G.O. Haller

On March 4, Wells sent Haller a copy of his letter to the Secretary of War, dated March 3, 1863. Haller proposed to some Masonic friends to have the matter investigated but was strongly advised against it. Haller wrote the following in response to Wells' letter of March 3.

Camp near Falmouth, VA
March 20th, 1863

C.H. Wells, Lieut. Commander, U.S.N.:

My dear sir: Your letter of March 4th, enclosing a copy of your letter to the Hon. E.M. Stanton, Secretary of War, reporting me "for uttering disloyal sentiments in my presence" is received. I have now waited over two weeks to learn what course the War Department would pursue on your statements- perhaps you can tell. They have not even asked for an application.
It is due to myself to say, that in passing through Washington, on the 25th of February, I called on Major Whiting and showed him your letters, and a copy of mine to you of February 19th, in which I promised or assumed that he would make a statement which I had promised to forward to you. He then offered to write one, and as I would leave the next morning too early to get it, he was to forward it to me here. He returned on the 5th inst., and on the 6th called at my tent and state that he had forgotten to write. Having stated to you masonically that I thought when he was called upon, he would give you a statement which would remove the hallucination under which you seem to labor. I was entitled as a Mason to a hearing; but your haste indicates rather an over-zealous desire to open a correspondence with the Honorable Secretary of War, than conform to obligations and preserve your honor and character from a foul blot. I take it for granted that the Secretary of War will refer your letter to Major Whiting, and I trust will allow me to be heard in the case. I feel safer

in his hands then I am sorry to say, I would in yours, and the day will come I trust, when I can have this matter investigate by the Masonic Lodge in York, and your conduct sifted and stamped as it deserves.

In your letter of Feb. 20th you write, "I shall not dwell upon personal allusions as the matter has, in my opinion, taken an official character." This may be your opinion, but the society in which I have been schooled for the last twenty-three years does not allow an officer or gentleman to accept the hospitalities of another as a friend and then go off and comment on what he has seen or heard to that friend's prejudice: much less can he cover himself with his official character when he is not there in his official capacity. But aside from the violations of hospitality and courtesy, there is a question of veracity in your statement.

I have heretofore abstained from commenting on your conduct and your lectures to me, in your letters, from the motives of delicacy. I had no wish to lend myself in any way to produce an open rupture of our social relations. You must do me the justice to admit in your heart, that you have thrust this issue upon me. You have repeatedly thrust at me your charges of disloyalty, after I told you that I would not ask you to take my own statements, but agreed to leave it to one who saw all, heard all, and knew all that took place. You will yet learn that your statement to the Honorable Secretary of War is false.

It is now my turn to lecture you a little and hold up to your gaze a few reflections of your own, for I hold that the old truism "Actions speak louder than words," is a self-evident fact, and by this test I am prepared to compare our Patriotism.

You saw me in Fredericksburg hasten to the wounded man and aiding there. You know that I volunteered, (When my duties excused me from service which might expose my person to danger,) to furnish one hundred men of my own command and stay with them to fix the R.R. Bridge, because two hundred men that day fled from that duty[16]. You know too that I am in the field and that Generals Burnside and Hooker have retained me in my old position under Gen. McClellan, and they at least are satisfied with my loyalty and the discharge of my duties.

---

[16] Brig. Gen. Herman Haupt, supervisor of the construction and transportation of the military railroads, told Haller that 200 soldiers and workers had abandoned their work of a railroad bridge, during the battle of Fredericksburg. Haller replied that he would supply 100 men of the 93rd NY Infantry, if approved by Gen. Burnside and would personally stay there and make sure none would quit or allow the workmen to leave either. Documentation has not been found if Haller's offer was accepted.

How is it with you? Your patriotism stands mostly on paper. In your letter of January 16th you write: "that I had been away a year." (Now think of it, you were "away a year!" Why, thousands of volunteers left their homes, with business unsettled, and have been away two years!) and for the sake of my family (think, too, you have said you are ready "to sacrifice your son," yet your family prevents you doing your duty, for you say) "I would prefer going to see in these exciting times, although my naval friends tell me that I have done my share. I think not, for I believe that no officer can do too much to assist in crushing this sinful rebellion." Here then, family considerations are acknowledge to have crushed out your patriotism, for you think that you have not done your share—that you cannot do too much. While you here admit that loyalty and patriotism require your services at sea, yet you have sought at the Navy Department for the order placing you in a peaceful station. This is your boasted loyalty, and in your letter of February 17, you say: "no one can doubt my loyalty." I have found, by experience, that most sanctimonious members of a church—those who intrude their religious feelings on all around them—are the most hypocritical, and have motives for displaying their outward piety. The truly pious man retires to the inner closet and there offers up his devotions. He lets his conduct speak of his moral qualities. So in all relations, I look at a man's actions, not at his professions and boastings, and make up my mind. In your letter of February 17, written from the quiet Navy Yard at Philadelphia, your patriotism reaches the climax. You say: When we are engaged in a deadly struggle to sustain (I suppose you unintentionally omitted the words "the constitution of") our government, I would sacrifice my son." Had this passage been prepared at sea, while devoting your life as a sacrifice, if necessary, to your bleeding country, it might pass for noble patriotism (although repugnant to our animal instincts, and evincing a most unnatural frame of mind,) but, while you take such good care of your own life, it sounds very much like a buncombe[17]!

Before that God, whom you profess to worship—who knows our hearts—and who understands our motives—I can fearlessly submit my loyalty and yours, and ask him to judge between us.

There are several passages in your letters, which might be noticed in addition to those above. But enough of this. I trust that I

---

[17] Definition: insincere or foolish talk; Buncombe County, N.C.; from a remark made by its congressman, around 1820, who defended a dull speech by claiming that he was speaking to Buncombe. A variant of the word bumkin.

may be able soon to get to York, and there I can get an investigation which will decide how far your charges of disloyalty go, and disinterested brethren judge between us.

Very respectfully, your obedient servant,
G.O. Haller,
Major 7th Infantry

The following is an application, written by Haller, requesting an official investigation of the charges brought about by Wells.

York, Pa.
August 8th, 1863

Hon. Edwin M. Stanton, Secretary of War,

Sir: on the 29th ult., I received a copy of Special Orders No. 331, which informed me that, "by the direction of the President" I was "dismissed from the service of the United States for disloyal conduct and the utterance of disloyal sentiments."

By this order I am deprived of the profession for which my education and lifelong habits have fitted me, and I am driven from it, covered with whatever of infamy the recorded condemnation of the highest authority can bring on my character. The statements which brought this about, being untrue, I hope it is not too late to get justice. At all events, I take the liberty to give you a true statement of my case, which, perhaps, may serve me in place of that regular defense which I have had no opportunity to make. Some vindication of myself I certainly owe to my family and my friends.

Undoubtedly an order which my consign an officer to ruin and disgrace, ought to be placed on specific and intelligible grounds. "Disloyal conduct" and "disloyal sentiments" are phrases unknown to any law civil or military, and have come into fashion of late, as mere party catch words, signifying anything or nothing, according to the notions of the persons who use them.

That I am or have been really disloyal in word, thought, or deed, is utterly and nakedly false. From the time I first entered the army, nearly twenty-four years ago, I have been true and faithful to my country, her government, her constitution and her laws. And this avertment never has been, and never will be controverted by the testimony of any man who is honest and sane. My services vouch for this. I was in much of the Florida war: through all the Mexican war, and in most of the battles from Palo Alto to El Molino Del Rey and Capture of the City of Mexico inclusive. I was engaged in several Indian Wars on the Pacific Coast and elsewhere, and in this Rebellion from its commencement until notified of my dismissal. I have never failed in the performance of any duty however difficult or dangerous, and I have never been charged with a single act of insubordination. I think I can say without boasting that I have enjoyed far beyond many officers the friendship of my associates and the approbation of my superiors in the service. The official reports on file in your Department, and printed in the Congressional Documents, will not only show this, but will prove that my behavior in every important battle, won from the Commanding Officers, expressions of the highest praise. I speak with the pride which becomes a solider, when I say that my record is without stain.

Almost contemporaneously with the bas accusations of Wells, Major General Burnside was writing the warmest eulogium on my fidelity to the cause of the Union: and only a few days before my dismissal, Major General Couch gave me the strongest evidence of his confidence, and of the high appreciation in which he held what he was pleased to call "the invaluable assistance" I had rendered him, in retarding the advance of the enemy in their march toward Philadelphia.

I am not now, I have never been, and it is likely I never will be a Politician. That is not my trade! I have interfered in no canvass, have written nothing for newspapers, and spoken at no public meetings. But I have held opinions on Public Affairs which, as they do not change when the civil administration changes, are sometimes favorable and sometimes unfavorable to the party in power. To these opinions, I have occasionally, in the freedom of private conversation, given moderate, fair, and inoffensive expression. This non-intervention in the political disputes of the people is the custom of service among the best officers of the Regular Army, and I have followed it because it has the approbation of my judgment and my conscience: and this freedom of opinion has been conceded to officers of the Army from the foundation of this Republic, and never has been questioned until now.

One Clark H. Wells, a Lieutenant Commander in the U.S. Navy, had a conversation with Major Charles J. Whiting, 2nd U.S. Cavalry, and myself, on or about the 17th December, 1862, (over seven months ago,) at my tent, on the Rappahannock, in which politics were mentioned, and it is upon his false and perverted statements of that private conversation that my dismissal is grounded. Those statements were referred to some subordinate in your office, and upon those alone I was found guilty of disloyalty, reported for dismissal, and actually dismissed. I now appeal to your sense of justice and ask you whether that is the fair play to which an officer of twenty fours years' service, with an unblemished record, is entitled? Who, in the army is safe, if the War Department opens its ear to the base whispers of every paltry spy, who treacherously takes advantage of an officer's hospitality and becomes an informer to curry favor with the dispensers of patronage? Apart from the individual wrong with such a practice must produce, can anything be better calculated to demoralize the Army and bring the service, as well as the Government itself, into disrepute?

Conversations are proverbially unreliable as evidence. They are so easily misunderstood, and so difficult to remember that there is not one instance in many thousands where the casual talk of a man can be reproduced with accuracy even by respectable witness. Nay, where is the man who can repeat exactly what he himself has said but yesterday? If conversations are of small accounts when detailed with all possible fairness, they become contemptible when tattled by a man of weak understanding and malicious heart.

I here aver that I never uttered the words imputed to me by Wells, nor any words of similar import, either at the time he refers to, or at any other time in my life. He says I drank to a Southern Confederacy during this Administration. This is merely and simply false, I can prove my denial to be true by the direct testimony of Major Whiting, (before mentioned,) a gentleman whose honor and veracity no one who knows him will doubt. The only toast given by me on that occasion was this: "Here's to the Constitution as it is, and the Union as it was!" which I thought then and think now, expresses a sentiment perfectly patriotic and most purely loyal.

Why did Mr. Wells make this false statement? Let me tell you. This man is crazy. Yes: the witness upon whose ex-parte statements your department has endeavored to bring ruin to me and my family is a lunatic! It was only on the 11th of October, 1861, that he was released from the Pennsylvania Hospital for the Insane at Philadelphia, and the act was accompanied by the written regret of the Medical Officer in charge, at seeing him leave before he was entirely well. I have know him for a long time; on my return to Camp, near Falmouth, Va., from York, Pa., he asked to accompany me to see an intimate friend. He was there not merely as my guest, but a self-invited guest, and under the greater obligations to respect the hospitality.

On the occasion to which his statements refer, he drank some punch, not excessively but enough to inflame his weak brain and aggravate his mental disease, which gradually irritated his morbid temper, and fixed his malice upon myself. He imagined that I had insinuated an unmanly fear on his part in crossing the Rappahannock river, during the firing of the enemy. He asked Major Whiting, whom he had met for the first time, to let him (Wells) sleep in his (Whiting's) tent, and insisted upon doing so while Major Whiting was advising him against it. It was in this manner I offered to find him a tent to sleep in where he would be with a Black Republican—not as he says I did. Although the moment before, he had denounced Southern chivalry, and their institution of Slavery as wrong and a curse, he became particularly incensed at this offer and invited himself into a stranger's tent. The next day, of his own accord, he came to my tent and begged me to say nothing more about the matter. His conduct and language for a long time afterwards did not indicate that the fancies excited by the punch had passed into settled hallucinations. On the contrary, when he left the Camp and returned to York where my family lived, he saw them, told them all about me, wrote an account of their health, and even cautioned me not to speak unguardedly on political subjects "lest some civilian might take advantage of it to injure me." When he wrote me at a still later period that he intended to accuse me of disloyalty for toasting the Southern Confederacy, I did my best to deter him until I could convince him, through Major Whiting, that he was in error. I knew he was not a responsible creature and I could feel no enmity towards him. But all my efforts to reason with him only strengthened his mental delusion, and intensified the insane malignity with which he had come to regard me.

Mr. Wells is not without that cunning which usually accompanies madness. Since his release from the Lunatic Asylum, he has taken all occasions, in season and out of season, to make his devotion to the administration conspicuous. But this is all feigned, for, if what he said when the war began is any indication of his mind, he must be a confirmed secessionist. He pushes his fortunes and tries to win promotion by threatening men with false accusations—always where he thinks it is his interest to do so—and several persons (among them his near relations) have been put in serious peril by his machinations. Thus far he has been remarkably successful. It is a fact that this Lunatic, so recently from the mad house, and seemingly unfit to run at large, has been very recently appointed to the Commandant of the Navy Yard at Philadelphia.

When I was informed by Mr. Wells himself that he had made this accusation, I did not think it necessary to send in a defense for I had faith in the government of the Country which I had served so long, and I believed that before any action would be taken against me, I would be called upon for an explanation. I certainly had no fear that the War Department would proceed on the unsupported statement of a crazy man, when it was known that there was sane witness who could tell all about it. I however consulted friends and every one advised me that I should not notice the allegations nor make any exposure of my accuser until it became absolutely necessary. I could not foresee that the necessity might exist without my knowing it.

I have made no assertions here which I cannot prove if an opportunity be given me, either by documentary or oral evidence. The letters, I refer to, are in my possession, the official reports are on file, and the witnesses will be forthcoming.

I do not suppose that either you or the President understood the nature of my case. Your action was grounded on the report laid before you, and I respectfully request of you the privilege of proving before a Court of Inquiry, or properly authorized Court, that the report was made upon the false testimony of an incompetent and irresponsible witness, taken in a corner behind my back, and without the privilege to cross-examine. With these facts before you, I trust that, as an act of sheer justice to myself, an investigation will be ordered. If I shall succeed in this I will leave the rest with the utmost confidence in your hands.

I have the honor to be, very respectfully,
Your obedient Servant,
Granville O. Haller
(late Major 7th Infantry.)

Haller's friends and superiors wrote letters stating his loyalty and dedication to the Union cause.

Portland, Me.
September 27, 1863

My dear Major:

Yours of the 23d I received yesterday, also a copy of C. H. Wells' letter to the Secretary of War. I say without any hesitation, that upon the time referred to in his letter, you never proposed such a toast, as he says you did, or uttered any sentiments which a true lover of his country might not have uttered even as an officer of the army. I cannot recollect the whole conversation, but my recollection of the general tenor of it is very distinct, and I think Lieut Wells first got offended with you, upon your asking him why he had not crossed the pontoon bridge; which question was drawn from you by Wells insinuating that you had always remained at headquarters. You are at liberty to show this letter to any of your friends, and state publicly or in print, that I pronounce Lieut Wells statement in regard to you, in connection with my name, as false in spirit as well as letter.

Yours truly,
Chas. J. Whiting

Pottsville, PA., Oct. 23d, 1863
Major Granville O. Haller:

Dear Sir: It affords me great pleasure to say that during the time we were associated together in the military service of the country at Columbia and Wrightsville, you manifested great zeal in behalf of the best interests of the country, and was indefatigable in your efforts while aiding me to make such dispositions of my small force as would enable us to repel an attack of the rebel horde that marched against use from York. At no time did I hear you utter a disloyal word or sentiment. I believe then as I believe now, that your activity and anxiety to thwart the enemy was prompted by the purest and most patriotic motives. Certainly no one of my command questioned for a moment your patriotism or your sincerity.

My orders were to prevent the enemy from crossing the Susquehanna at or near Columbia at all hazards; and when the propriety of destroying the Columbia Bridge was being discussed, you joined with me that the best interests of the service—the safety of the Capitol of the State, as well as the preservation of Railroad communication between that point and Lancaster and Philadelphia, demanded its destruction.

In conclusion I have only to say that your conduct met, as it deserved, my approbation, and I have yet to hear of word of disparagement from those with whom you were associated.

Very respectfully, your Ob't. Serv't.,
Jacob G. Frick,
Late Col./129th Pa. Vols.,
And Col. 27th Pa. Vols. Militia

Gettysburg, Oct. 28, 1863

Maj. G.O. Haller:

Sir: It affords me pleasure to state that as a member of the Committee of Safety, appointed at a public meeting of citizens of this town, in June last, I was frequently at your quarters, and had knowledge of the efforts made by you to arrest or retard the progress of the rebel army on the borders of our county, by organizing the citizens as "Home Guards" and otherwise, and to testify to the zeal and earnestness manifested by you on the occasion, and that, so far as my observation extended, your conduct and conversation were uniformly such as became a loyal citizen and an officer of the United States Army.

Very respectfully yours,
R. G. McCreary

Gettysburg, PA., Oct. 28, 1863

Maj. G.O. Haller:

    Dear Sir: I fully concur with Mr. McCreary in the substance of the foregoing letter. In addition I take the liberty to add that I told you I was sorry to see the Democrats of our town did not attend the meeting called by our Committee of Safety, which meeting was held at your solicitation for the purpose of making arrangements for the organization of Home Guards for border defense. You suggested that you were of that political persuasion and wished to meet some of the prominent men of that party to endeavor to persuade them to unit in the efforts making to repel the invaders, and that they should fight the rebels first and after that they could attack the administration in a legitimate and constitutional way. I know that you made every effort to bring about a concert of action here for the purpose of organizing the Town and County for border defense.

I remain yours truly,
David Wills

Gettysburg, PA., Oct. 29, 1863

Major G.O. Haller:

    Major: It affords me great pleasure to be able to testify to the earnestness and zeal you displayed in June last, during the Rebel invasion. Having access to your room at all hours day and night, and in frequent confidential conversations with you, I have no hesitancy in saying you did everything you could as a loyal officer of the Government with the small and inaffective force you had at your disposal to retard the advance of the Rebels east of the South Mountain, and that I had no reason to doubt your loyalty whatever, and was very much surprised to hear of your being dismissed from the service. If I can be of any further service to you it will afford me great pleasure.

I am yours most obediently
Robert Bell,
Capt. Adams County Scouts,
(now Co. B, 21st P.V. Cav.)

Gettysburg, October 29th, 1863

    Sir[18]: Having been constantly in intercourse and actively co-operating with Major G.O. Haller, while on duty here in June last, as aid to Major Genl. D.N. Couch, Commanding the Dept. of the Susquehanna—I cheerfully state, that, Maj. Haller was constant and earnest in the discharge of his duties, at this post.
    Not only was their neither act nor expression proceeding from him, in any manner suggestive of disloyalty, but on the contrary his whole bearing and conduct here was characterized by zeal and activity as an officer. From my intimate knowledge of all that was transpiring, and the facts which furnished the basis of his action, I was strongly persuaded, that, his proceedings in advancing the 26th Regiment[19], (Col. Jennings), were justified by the information derived from Cavalry reconnoissances, and furnished him by the officers in charge of the scouting operations[20].
    With the limited force at his command, Major Haller's whole actions impressed me with the conviction that, he was seeking earnestly to do, all that he could, for the public service and the defeat of the enemy, and the thwarting the movements.
    As a citizen who felt a very intense interest for the success of the Arms of the Union and the rout of the Rebel forces; and, keenly alive to any thing, however slight, which might betray a want of loyalty in any one with whom I might be thrown in contact, I have no hesitation in thus strongly giving expression to the impressions made upon me in my intercourse with Major Haller.

---

[18] The addressee of this letter is unknown
[19] 26th Pennsylvania Militia Regiment
[20] After the Gettysburg Campaign Haller was accused by a Rev. M. Jacobs for sending the 26th Regiment into a trap, which would have resulted in its capture or destruction, if not for Col. Jennings assuming responsibility and leading the Regiment out of the trap. Facts show that it was Jennings who lead the Regiment into a position without orders and into its misfortunes.

Most respectfully and truly,
D. McConaughy[21]

---

[21] A member of the Gettysburg's Committee of Safety during the Gettysburg Campaign

IN DEFENSE OF MAJOR HALLER
Who was Major Haller? Here is his background in his own and others words.

Early years

I was an applicant for the appointment of Cadet in the Military Academy at West Point in 1839, but having turned my twentieth year[22], I received an invitation to appear to a Military board[23], which convened in the City of Washington, to examine the qualifications of young men who desired to be commissioned as Officers; and having passed a satisfactory examination, I received from President Martin Van Buren, through the Hon. Joel R. Poinsett, Secretary of War, a Commission with the rank of Second Lieutenant in the 4th Regiment of Infantry, from the 17th day of November, 1839[24].

In 1840, I joined my Regiment at Fort Gibson, a very sickly post, in the Cherokee Nation of Indians.

The Florida War[25]

In 1841, Regiment entered Florida the second time. My company formed part of Major Belknap's column which explored and scouted the Big Cypress Swamp. In this expedition all the Officers and men had to carry knapsacks, as the country was impractical for horses or mules. Each one carried his change of clothing, blankets, and seven days' rations, and had to wade daily in the water from the ankle to waist deep, but mostly about twelve inches deep—in stretches of usually eight or ten mile—in the cold weather of December. On the 20th December 1841, the Indians in this swamp

---

[22] Haller was born on January 31, 1819 in York, PA to George and Susan Haller His father died when he was two years old and his mother had hoped he would study for the ministry

[23] Because a clerk of the House of Representatives, who was also a friend of then Senator James Buchanan of Pennsylvania, had recently died, Buchanan strongly urged that the clerk's son should get the appointment. The name of the clerk's son was William Franklin who would later command the Union's Sixth Army Corps

[24] Because of his direct commission he out ranked the graduating class of 1840 and those who would have been in his class of 1843

[25] This is the Second Seminole War, 1835-1842; the First Seminole War was from 1817-1818 and the lesser known Third Seminole War was from 1856-1858

fired upon our column while in the water three feet deep, killing several men[26].

In 1842, as Acting Adjutant of my Regiment, I served with the expedition under Col. Worth which scouted the Wahoo Swamp, then crossed the Palalikaha River, where his troops surprised Halleck Tustenugge in his camp with all of the women and children of the tribe about him, and obliged him to fight, to give time to the non-combatants to escape. The lodges, clothing and dried meats, etc. fell into our hands, after a sharp skirmish, in which they had several warriors wounded. This misfortune obliged Halleck to sue for peace, which was soon followed by the suspension of Indian hostilities. The Regiment was then sent to Jefferson Barracks, Missouri.

In 1844, my Regiment was ordered into Louisiana and encamped near Nachetoches, on the borders of Texas, as part of the "Army of Observation,"[27] as Mexico had threatened Texas with invasion on account of her negotiating terms of annexation with the United States.

In 1845, the 3rd and 4th Regiments of Infantry became the "Army of Occupation" and took possession of St. Joseph's Island and Corpus Christi, Texas. I was here appointed "Brigade Major" of the 3rd Brigade, a title now obsolete, as the duty is performed by the Assistant Adjutant General.

The Mexican War

In 1846, the "Army of Occupation" marched to the Rio Grande and encamped opposite Matamoros. I was here appointed the Commissary of 3rd Brigade. At Point Isabella I was ordered to receive and receipt for all the subsistence stores, which the train of wagons would be able to carry to Fort Brown. Returning, the enemy met us at Palo Alto, on the 8th of May, and disputed our passage, but had to fall back; on the 9th the enemy held a stronger position, and fought the battle of Resaca De La Palma, and sustained heavy losses, and defeat. A large quantity of their subsistence stores, was captured, and placed in my charge. On the field, I acted as an Aid-de-Camp to Lt. Col. John Garland, 4th Infantry, commanding the 3rd Brigade, and in his

---

[26] This was his first action in combat
[27] The Army of Observation was about 4,000 soldiers and was commanded by General Zachary Taylor

report of those actions, he as expressed his indebtedness to me for valuable assistance.

When the Army marched to Monterey, in addition to the duties of Commissary of 3rd Brigade, I was charged with the duties of Quartermaster and Commissary to Gen. Twiggs' Division. Immediately on our arrival before Monterey, I was ordered to take charge of all the subsistence that had been brought to that place, with instructions to be sparing in the issues, and by judicious distributions, protracted the subsistence until fresh supplies were received. I was kept on commissary duty until Gen. Worth's Division was withdrawn from Saltillo, to join Gen. Scott's column. Before embarking for Vera Cruz, Gen. Worth directed Company Commanders, who were also doing Staff duty, to select one of the two duties which they preferred, and surrender the other. I thereupon retained command of my Company, and turned my Staff duty to Lieut. Grant[28], of my Regiment.

At Vera Cruz, Gen. Worth's Division was charged with the construction of certain trenches, and my Regiment worked both night and day, then furnished guards for them. Our labors were incessant until the City capitulated.

At Cerro Gordo, my Regiment was part of the Reserve, but witnessed and participated in the success of that day.

The Castle of Perote and the City of Puerla fell without a blow, but the 4th Infantry formed part of the column sent to reduce those places.

In the Valley of Mexico, my Regiment participated in all the battles. At El Molino Del Rey, I was one of the "Storming Party"[29] being selected as one of the officers to bring on the assault. In the capture of the City of Mexico, our last blow, my conduct seems to have met the decided approbation of my superior officers.

For my services in Mexico, I received two commissions by Brevet. The first one was the rank of Captain by Brevet, from the 8th Sept., 1847 "for gallant and meritorious conduct in the battle of Molino Del Rey." The second was the rank of Major by Brevet, from

---

[28] Ulysses Grant who later rose to command all Union forces during the Civil War; Grant also served a tour at Vancouver Barracks, Washington Territory in 1852

[29] The commanding officer of the Storming Party was Capt., later Brig. Gen., George Wright

the 13th Sept., 1847 "for gallant and meritorious conduct in the battle of Chapultepec, Mexico." [30]

Services on the Pacific slope

In 1852, my Company embarked on the US steamship *Fredonia*[31], sailed around Cape Horn, and after a seven month voyage, reached San Francisco, thence sailed in a steamer to Fort Vancouver, Washington Territory, and shortly after, July 1853, was stationed at Fort Dalles, Oregon, then a Territory, a dreary, isolated spot, but since has become a thriving city, in consequence of the developments of the gold region to the east of it. In those days freight from Portland to the Dalles (one hundred miles) was $75.00 per ton: the ordinary necessities of a family, far exceeded an officer's pay: luxuries were scarcely to be had—eggs 12 ½ cents each, butter $1.50 per pound, contract price of beef 27 cents per pound, etc. At that time it was indeed, mentally as well as peculiarly, a great trail to be confined to a post so destitute of all that makes life agreeable.

Letter below is extracted from Henrietta Haller to her mother Charlotte Cox after their arrival at Fort Vancouver, late June or early July 1853

My dear Mama, We have at last arrived at the end of – I hope, our journey by sea, and have reached Fort Vancouver safely, thank God! I will tell you, as well as I can, all that happened since leaving Lima [Peru]. We had delightful weather till we neared San Francisco and we had a very pleasant time. The only person that made trouble were the Rains faction. They have a horrible servant girl who is "commanding officer" and rules them all. The Major had several men confined on her account. He had changed orders so often to please her that the men could not keep track of them and, in obeying what they

---

[30] On April 10, 1849 both the House and Senate of the State of Pennsylvania passed a resolution thanking those members of the military, and a citizen of the state, who distinguished themselves in the war with Mexico. Haller was one of those recognized.

[31] The rest of the regiment had sailed in late June 1852 and arrived in Oregon Territory and arrived in September; Haller's company sailed in November. At this time the main forts of the Territory were Fort Vancouver (on the Columbia River) established 1849, Fort Steilacoom (on Puget Sound) established 1849, and Fort Dalles (in eastern Oregon and near the Columbia River) established 1848.

thought was the last order, interfered with Miss Sarah Sweet. She was constantly scolding and fighting and the officers requested Major Rains to put her out of the Mess. But he would not.

We are ordered to the Dalles—a place where there are not quarters at all and we will have to wait till they are built. And, worst of all, that abominable Major Rains is to command. I believe that there is a curse on all that he does, and those that are with him. After all the perils and troubles of our voyage to have an end like this!

Letter below is extracted from Henrietta Haller to her sister Ellen Cox, Fort Dalles, August 28, 1853

My dear Ellen, Our quarters are built of logs—I absolutely had written brick!—chinked with mud, which keeps constantly falling out. We can see through them above, below and at the ends. I can now hear every word of the conversation carried on in Dr. Summer's room, which is next to mine. We have two rooms and will have a kitchen when it can be built—and there is no lumber. There is a crazy old saw mill here with a warped saw and leaking dam which Major Rains insists upon repairing and working though the lumber will cost the government twice as much as if it was bought, besides working the men to death to repair it. Mr. Montgomery—the Quartermaster—asked him to let him buy lumber for necessary repairs here; he refused to allow it for he had enough for himself and does not care if we all die of want of shelter or comfort.

Massacre on Boise River

In 1854, the family of a Mr. Ward[32], and other immigrants, were massacred on Boise River, about three hundred and fifty-five miles from the Dalles, by the Winneste Indians[33], a tribe of the great Shoshone Nation, under circumstances of the most atrocious barbarity[34].

The two companies then at Fort Dalles, were reduced by discharges and desertions to fifty-six soldiers all told. I was dispatched with twenty-six of them to the massacre ground, there to

---

[32] This was a group of 20 emigrants, on the Oregon Trail and Alexander Ward was one of the members. It is known as the Ward massacre
[33] This tribe was also known as the White Knives
[34] Haller and his command found that all but 2 boys were killed and most died in a horrible way including children being burned alive

chastise the murderers and give protection to the immigrants. The citizens of, and the immigrants at the Dalles, thinking my small force inadequate, formed a company of thirty-nine volunteers, followed after me, and reported for duty. At the Grande Ronde (one hundred and ninety miles from the Dalles) a few warriors of the Nez Perce and Umatilla Indians offered their services to me and were accepted. With this mixed force we invade the usual haunts of the murderers, killed a few, and recaptured the clothing and other effects taken from their victims. With an old Indian, some squaws and children, captives, we brought up the road of the immigration. In the correspondence between Brig. Gen. John E. Wool, commanding the Department of the Pacific, and the then Secretary of War, Jefferson Davis, which was published by the US Senate, I found the latter had expressed his approval, in strong terms, of my services and energy in this expedition.

Letter below is extracted from Henrietta Haller to her sister Ellen Cox, Fort Dalles, April 9, 1854

My dear Ellen, I think we need not be under any apprehension about the Indians here, for they are not able, if they were willing, to hunt us. The Nez Perce's and the Cayuses are powerful and warlike but they are to the whites, tho' not to the Wascoes and Wishrams about here. The whites are too necessary to the Indians in trading and in various ways for them to wish to get rid of them, we think.

We had one panic, but that was Major Rain's fancies. He is the vilest coward on earth and besides is crazy every now and then on some subject or other. The only thing he never loses sight of is his own interest and everything must give way to that. Anybody that would put anything in his pocket or his greedy mouth can do what they please. The whole family is intolerable liars that the best way to come at the truth is to believe the opposite of everything they say. He has kept nearly all the carpenters at the Post working at his quarters since the 4th of July last.

Second Snake Indian[35] Expedition

In 1855, General Wool organized a force of over one hundred and fifty men, and placed me in command, to further chastise these murderers. Returning to Fort Boise in the fishing season, we drove the guilty Indians from their fishing places on Boise and Payette rivers, then advanced some five hundred miles from Fort Dalles, and established a depot on the Big Camash Prairie, from whence we scouted the head-waters of Boise, Payette, and Salmon rivers, on the north of us, and to the Rocky Mountains and head-waters on the Missouri, on the east, and at Salmon Falls and along the Snake River on the south. In this expedition we hung several of the murderers over the graves of their victims[36]; in the mountains we hung and killed others, until we had destroyed as many warriors as they had killed of the whites, besides having captured women and children and old men. The remnant of the tribe fled in terror towards Humboldt River in California. In this expedition some of our horsed had travelled at least seventeen hundred miles.

Headquarters Department of the Pacific [extract]
Benicia, September 4, 1855

Sir: I have reports from Brevet Major Haller, commanding the expedition against the Snake Indians, dated July 31.
The command reached Fort Boise July 15, Mr. Olney, Indian agent, being with it. The next day a talk was held with some two hundred Indians there collected, of whom sixty-five were warriors; and it having been ascertained that four of the murderers were present, they were seized, brought before a board of officers, or, as Major Haller terms it, a military commission, and, their guilt having been clearly established, three were hung on the graves of their victims, the 18th; the fourth was shot by the guard in endeavoring to escape. The proceedings of the commission are herewith enclosed.

---

[35] The US Army and travelers along the Oregon Trail often had problems with the Snake Indians; by February 1863 the Army had established and manned Ft. Boise. From this post a series of expeditions would be launched against the Snakes over the next few years.

[36] Haller and his command had a meeting with the Indian tribes around the Boise River area and it was found out that several of those in attendance participated in the Ward massacre. Haller ordered them arrested, formed a military commissioned, tried and hanged them at the massacre site

The command then continued to the great Cammish prairie, thirty-five miles west from crossing of Malade river, and upwards of sixty miles beyond Fort Boise. One emigrant train had been met and escorted to Fort Boise, and detachments had been sent out towards the Salmon falls, and other routes where emigrants were expected, and where they might be molested by the Indians.

It appears that a tribe known as the White-knives, numerous and powerful, are the authors and instigators of most of the outrages committed by Indians upon emigrants, their object being plunder. They cover a large extent of country along the south side of Snake river for one hundred miles above and below the Salmon falls, across to the headwaters of Humboldt river, and down that stream, and across to Lake Syloi, at or near the head of Malheur river. It was Major Haller's purpose to visit this tribe, and to cut them off from their fishery. He had some expectation of a hostile reception from them.

The activity and energy of Major Haller, and the officers of his command, deserve commendation.

I am, sir, very respectfully, your obedient servant,
John E. Wool, Major General

Effects Of Gold Discoveries

About this time, the discoveries of gold by the employees of the Hudson Bay Company, near their trading post, Fort Colville, in Washington Territory, became well known, and caused many miners to visit that region; many passing from Puget Sound through the Klikatat and Yakima Country, and, in the latter, two or more miners were murdered. Having ordered my command to return to the Dalles, I proceeded in advance by rapid marches, and found a threatening state of affairs to exist quite close to Fort Dalles. The Indian tribes were sullen and hostile, and the whites much excited. Major Bolan[37], a highly esteemed citizen of Washington Territory, and Sub-Indian Agent in charge of the Yakimas, went to this tribe to counsel them for

---

[37] Sub-agent Andrew Bolan had planned to visit with Washington Territorial Governor Issac Stevens but instead went into Yakima country to investigate the death of miners. In 1918 the Washington State Historical Society put up two markers 11 miles northwest of Goldendale, Washington in honor of Agent Bolan. The 76 year-old son of Gov. Stevens, Hazard Stevens, was there at the dedication; Hazard collapsed shortly after starting his speech and died a few days later.

peace and to get the murderers. He was assassinated. The Indians knew very well that if the death of their Agent became known to the troops, immediate war would follow. They therefore sent runners to inform their allies of their danger, and threw out scouts to observe the movements of the soldiers at Fort Dalles, and took every precaution to keep those Indians not disposed for war, from communicating with the white people.

The Oregon War

The long absence of Major Bolan from the Dalles, caused me to send an Indian spy in the Yakima district to learn something about him. It was with difficulty he could get back. In the meantime an old squaw escaped through their lines and brought the news of Bolan's assassination, and the collection of warriors from all the neighboring tribes to wipe out the white people. The information was confirmed in various ways, and it was duly communicated to the Commanding Officer of the District[38], stationed at Fort Vancouver. By this time the Infantry portion of my Battalion had arrived from the Camash prairie, and all the available force at Fort Dalles—making one hundred fighting me, divided into two companies, and one Sergeant Major, and one Commissary and Quartermaster Sergeant—total 102—having Captain Russell and myself commanding companies; Lieut. Gracie in charge of the mountain howitzer; and Asst. Surgeon George W. Hammond, as medical officer—were held in readiness, with subsistence, for the command, prepared the pack-mules, to march at a moment's notice. But this news brought me no orders to march.

Fortunately the Acting Governor of Washington Territory heard of the murders of the two miners, and made a requisition for one company of US troops to invade the Yakima Country from Fort Dalles and demand the murderers from that tribe. The Commandant of the District ordered me to send a company, but knowing the peril, I took the responsibility of taking all my available force, and went in person. A consciousness of the danger induced me to proceed with, not to send this little band of soldiers, and I believe that the Adjutant General of the US Army, will bear me witness that I have never sought to avoid necessary danger, but have always encountered the enemy and used my humble abilities to the best advantage for my country.

---

[38] Major Gabriel Rains commanding the Fourth Infantry

Three Days Of Fighting

    The first night out my spy returned having escaped from the hostile camp and declared that Kamiarkin[39], the Yakima Chief, had collected more warriors than he was able to designate by numbers, and that a force double the size of my command would never be able to get back. We however advanced and on the fourth day, as we descended a hill to the bottom lands of Topinish[40] Creek to encamp, we discovered the Indians taking position behind the trees to fight. At the same time, a chief on a distant bluff was making a harangue to his warriors, who replied to him with yell, and thus showed their positions and that they were not greatly superior in numbers. As soon as our mule train had come up and our rear was properly guarded, we attacked our adversaries and drove them off. During the action fresh warriors came up and showed themselves on the bluffs around us. At sundown perhaps six hundred warriors were in view but all retired during the twilight. Early the next morning the warriors surrounded our position but a few shots make them cautious, until they found our balls fell wide of their marks—we having only the old smooth bored muskets with spherical balls. In several instances war parties becoming more venturesome would crawl up very close to the knolls behind which our men awaited their approach, and would with stones construct what is now called rifle pits, to annoy our skirmishers when they exposed themselves, and these were driven off by bayonet charges.

    Our position enables us to see over the plain, and hourly fresh clouds of dust announced the approach of reinforcements to our foes. We had not rations enough to hold out until reinforcements from Fort Vancouver could join us, and it would have been as foolish as disastrous to attempt with my small force of foot soldiers to chastise or subdue the well mounted and active enemy before us. Prudence therefore made it my duty to return if practicable to Fort Dalles, where a properly mounted party would be organized to assist our efforts. Hence at night we retraced our steps to the top of the mountain near us, and allowed the men rest, and next morning fell back towards Fort Dalles, skirmishing with the Indians until nearly sundown. We lost five killed and seventeen wounded, and brought the

---

[39] The more standard spelling of this name is Kamiakin

[40] The modern spelling of this creek is Toppinish

wounded in safely, also the corpse of the gallant Commissary Sergeant Mulholland, who fell in the last bayonet charge[41].

The Commandant of the District being advised by courier of the defeat of my expedition, and the vast proportions that the war was likely to assume, called on the Governors of Oregon and Washington Territories, each, for two companies of volunteers.

Headquarters, Columbia River, Puget Sound District [extract]
Fort Vancouver, W.T., October 9, 1855

      Governor: We have just received the information from Brevet Major Haller, who was ordered into the Yakima country with a force of consisting of five officers, one hundred and two men, and one mountain howitzer, on the 3rd instant. He states that he fell in with the enemy on the afternoon of the 6th instant, and commenced an action with them in the brush of the Pisco river, and after fighting some time he drove them out at a point of the bayonet, and has taken possession of the heights surrounding the river. He was surrounded, and has called for reinforcements.

      This morning Lieutenant Day, of artillery, leaves Fort Dalles to join Major Haller's command, with about forty-five men and one mountain howitzer.

I am Governor, very respectfully, your obedient servant
G.J. Rains
Major 4th Infantry, Commanding

Headquarters Department of the Pacific [extract]
Benicia, California, October 19, 1855

      Sir: The Yakimas and Klikitats Indians, in Oregon and Washington Territories, being dissatisfied, it is said, with the treaty made with Governor Stevens, have assumed a warlike attitude, and having killed a number of white inhabitants going to and returning from the mines near Fort Colville. To punish these Indians, and to check their murderous intentions, Major Haller moved against them with about 100 men. He met them on the banks of the Pisco river,

---

[41] The expedition was from October 3-10. The total number of Indians surrounding Haller's command started with a few hundred; by the third day was estimated at over 1,000 and more were expected

Sinqua valley, but finding them too strong, he retired to the heights and sent for a reinforcement. Major Rains, with all the forces under his command, marched to his relief. I have ordered two detachments, one from Benicia and the other from the Presidio, composed of one captain, two lieutenants, and seventy rank and file, to proceed in the steamer *Columbia*, to reinforce Major Rains. I have no doubt the Major will be able to chastise the Indians and bring them to terms.

I am, very respectfully, your obedient servant,
John E. Wool, Major General

Headquarters, Territory of Oregon [extract]
Portland, October 24, 1855

  Sir: The frontiers of our Territory are again the scene of Indian hostilities. Heretofore, operations for their suppression have been directed against single tribes or combinations not formidable in point of numbers. The extent of the alliance, the numbers already openly in arms, and the character for bravery and perseverance of the allied tribes, render the present hostilities, especially on the northern frontier, exceedingly grave and important.
  Suspicion for some time past has been attracted towards the Yakimas and Klikitats, and the intercourse of the latter with the bands dispersed through the settlements in the valley of the Willamette has been very carefully observed. To what extent the tampering with these bands has been successful is not known, but the simultaneous rising of the Shasta and Rogue River Indians, in Southern Oregon, has occasioned an extraordinary feeling of alarm and insecurity throughout the whole extent of our settlements.
  A.J. Bolan, esq. one of the sub-Indian agents of Washington Territory, lately returned from the interior. Having heard that depredations were being committed by the Yakima upon parties of our citizens returning through their country from the Pend d'Oreilles mines, and that several returning miners had been waylaid and murdered, immediately set out for the camp of Ca-mi-a-kin, the principal chief, by appointment of Governor Stevens, relying for their own safety upon the friendly disposition always manifested towards him, and with a confident expectation of being able to reconcile, by his presence, any existing feeling of hostilities. On the way he was waylaid and most barbarously murdered by the orders of the treacherous Ca-mi-a-kin. His death signalized the general outbreak.

Brevet Major Haller, in command at Fort Dalles, with commendable promptitude and gallantry, commenced operations against the enemy; but the events of a few days ascertained the inadequacy of the whole disposable forces of the United States troops in the military district to suppress hostilities.

I am, very respectfully, your obedient servant,
Geo. L. Curry, Governor of Oregon

Major Gabriel Rains' Expedition

Gov. Curry[42], of Oregon Territory, believing that a respectable force sent into hostile country would keep the enemy occupied at their own homes watching after the safety of their women and children, and thus save the white settlements from rapine and murder, called out a regiment and commissioned the present Senator from Oregon, General Nesmith[43], as the Colonel but his commission being superior to the rank of the Major Commanding the District, the latter threw obstacles in the way of so large a force, apprehending the loss of command in the District. Some delay occurred and the winter weather overtook the troops in the enemy's country, and drove them back to the Dalles. It was not until Acting Governor of Washington Territory had called out two companies of volunteers and made the Commandant of the District Brigadier General of these two companies and such forces as should operated in his Territory, that the column was put in motion.

Our forces consisted of about three hundred regulars and about five hundred volunteer cavalry, well mounted, marched through a dangerous gorge in the mountains into the Yakima Valley, and found a few Indians upon the opposite side of the river, evidently bent on annoying us. The infantry was ordered across the river, but the water was so cold and swift that two men were chilled and unable to save themselves from drowning. Col. Nesmith then crossed with a troop of cavalry and routed the enemy without a casualty, except a trifling wound to his horse. Another portion of the cavalry had gone off in

---

[42] George L. Curry (1820-78), served as Governor of Oregon Territory, 1853, 1854; 1854-59; also served as a member of Oregon's territorial legislature and Secretary of Oregon Territory before becoming governor. Buried at the Lone Fir Cemetery in Portland, Oregon

[43] James W. Nesmith (1820-85), later became state court judge in Oregon; U.S. Senator from Oregon, 1861-67; U.S. Representative from Oregon at-large, 1873-75

another direction, to forage, and was fired upon by the Indians and had a few men wounded.

Next morning we could see distinctly masses of the Indians on the "Buttes" at the mouth of Attanem Creek, only a few miles off, and some of the braves came up quite close to our camp. Our General estimated the enemy at three hundred warriors, yet these braves disputed the passage at the "Buttes" until so late an hour that our command went into camp without dislodging them. Our General then invited the best marksmen to go out to the "Butte" in front, and have "a free fight" with the Indians on the hill, but our men were soon driven into camp in confusion. My company instantly sprang to their arms and covered the retreating party. I learnt from them that the Indians had come down into the timber on the river bank, and had opened a fire on their flank. Immediately my company charged the wood and followed the Indians up hill and drove them off the "Butte" without a casualty. As I advanced, I found Captain Augur's company supporting my movement. The Indians gave up the field for the night, but, early in the morning, attempted to resume their position on the "Butte." However they were quickly dislodged, and one of them was killed by a friendly Indian who had gone with me through all my Indian campaigns. Soon after, snow began to fall, and our campaign came to an inglorious end. This was my third campaign, in the six months preceding, the first of which exceeded fifteen hundred miles of travel.

Colonel George Wright's Campaign

Col. Wright, with his regiment, the 9th Infantry[44], but armed with the Minnie rifle, a short time after Brigadier General Rains' expedition, arrived at Fort Vancouver, and assumed command of the District. Gov. Curry, of Oregon Territory, seeing an adequate force of US troops now ready to take the field, withdrew his volunteers.

The arduous services performed by my company in the three expeditions of 1855, induced Col. Wright to let it rest and garrison Fort Dalles, while he, in the Spring of 1856, marched with his available force against the hostile Indians. He had provided that one company of his regiment should garrison Fort Vancouver and another

---

[44] The 9th Infantry, from Fort Monroe, VA was sent to reinforce the Department of the Pacific sometime after December 1, 1855 because of General Wool's request for more troops

guard the portage at the Cascades of the Columbia River, and as two other companies were operating on Puget Sound, it left him only six companies and a troop of cavalry with which to erect several posts in the enemy's country and also scout and chastise the Indians—he consequently had no soldiers to spare from his expedition. The transportation on the Columbia River being very limited, for the increase of business brought on by the war, it too time to get the companies to Fort Dalles, and just as the company designated to protect the portage at the Cascades, was about to move, General Wool, made a flying visit in the mail steamer to Fort Vancouver, and finding the two companies there took them off at once to Puget Sound, beyond Col. Wright's control, without ascertaining what effect it might have on the Colonel's plans. To replace these losses in the Colonel's rear was to weaken and destroy his efficiency in the field. He therefore trusted the portage to a Sergeant and a few men of the 4th Infantry and commenced his march. The hostile Indians, knowing the movement had commenced, sprang upon the settlement at the Cascades, and compelled the hitherto friendly Indians to join with them in killing men, women and children, and burning houses. One of the steamers barely escaped capture. The soldiers defend their blockhouse and some families near by, and at the upper extremity of the portage, all the citizens, who could, rallied in a larger storehouse, and there made a gallant defense. As soon as the news reached the Dalles that night, Col. Wright was notified, and the next morning his command returned and took passage for the Cascades, where he encountered the enemy and soon routed them.

    The several tribes around the Dalles still friendly, brought in their arms and proved the sincerity of their friendship by depositing them in my charge, and thus relieved from apprehension the minds of the white inhabitants. The Indians elsewhere, hitherto friendly, were surprised at the success against the whites, and joined the war party. Besides the serious loss of life and property at the Cascades, and detention and change of plan of Colonel Wright's expedition, the enemy became more confident and daring. Near the Nachess River, they were drawn up in position to oppose Colonel Wright's[45] progress

---

[45] In 1858 Col. Wright led a force of 700 troops against the Indians of what is now eastern Washington and northern Idaho. This highly successful campaign ended all thoughts of any more Indian uprisings, against the whites, in Washington Territory. Later he became commander, in 1864, of the Department of the Pacific and drowned on his way to command the newly formed Department of the Columbia in 1865

into their country. Their force had to be respected, and the Colonel thought it prudent to draw every available soldier from Fort Dalles to join him, so my company again took the field. A battalion of three companies was placed in my charge, and with this force I accompanied him on his long march through the hostile territory, north of the Dalles. Finally, I was left in the Kit-e-tas Valley to keep out the hostile Indians, until orders were received from General Wool, in the fall of the year, for my company to proceed to Puget Sound.

Fort Townshend[46]

While I was in camp in the Kit-e-tas Valley, I was ordered by General Wool, with my company, to Puget Sound. I received orders, also, before leaving, from the Commandant of the Puget Sound District, Lieut. Col. S. Casey[47], 9th Inf., to procure at Fort Vancouver the necessary building materials and implements, for constructing a military post, and to land my company near the village of Port Townsend, in Washington Territory, and if I approved of the site already chosen for the fort, to proceed to clearing the land of its timber, and construct quarters. After a reasonable time my officers and soldiers were provided with comfortable barracks, but the labor was severe and immense, to clear the timber away in a dense forest—trees from three to six feet in diameter, and nearly two hundred feet high—grade the ground, etc. Yet I had to superintend the work, be my own pioneer in the woods, my own architect to design the plans of the buildings, my own Quartermaster and Commissary of Subsistence, and do the duty of Lieutenants, for those promoted to my company had not then joined. Mr. George Gibbs of Washington Ty., came to my assistance and relieved me very much. The change from the excitement of the field service to constant hard labor was a trying one to soldiers. The discovery of rich gold fields, on Fraser River, offered strong temptations to the soldiers to desert to British Columbia. There never was a time when more vigilance was required of one company officer, and I am sure that no officer ever gave more faithful services to his country than I did at Fort Townshend.

---

[46] Haller means Fort Townsend which is now a Washington State park located just south of the present day town of Port Townsend

[47] Silas Casey, during the Civil War, fought at the Battle of Seven Pines and which Casey's Redoubt is named after. He also served as president of a board to examine candidates for officers of Negro troops and wrote the book *Infantry Tactics* which was adopted by the government

San Juan Island

The Department of Oregon[48] was formed in 1859 and assigned to Brig. Gen. Harney[49]. He soon altered the face of things, direction posts, that had just been constructed, to be abandoned, and new ones established elsewhere. Ignoring the instructions of the Secretary of State, Mr. Marcy, to the Governor of Washington Territory, to abstain further exercise of authority on San Juan Island until the water boundary between the United States and the British Possessions should be determined by competent authority—and commissioners were then engaged in adjusting this very live—he sent the company from Fort Bellingham (just abandoned) to take possession of San Juan Island and suspend British authority there, and substitute that of the United States. Captain Pickett[50], commanding, issued a proclamation to this effect in orders. The authorities of British Columbia were highly incensed at it, and too measures to collect all their available forces near the Island, and might have plunged the two countries immediately in war, but for an insignificant incident, and, as they had five formidable war vessels in the waters of British Columbia, they might have suspended, if not destroyed our immense commercial interests on the Pacific Coast, before the authorities in Washington could be appraised of the trouble—for there was then no telegraph across the continent as now.

The incident alluded to, was the arrival of our mail bring European news, but, particularly, the battle of Solferino. The British officers first heard of this battle from us, as their mails had failed to arrive. It occurred to them that Mr. Dallas, our Minister in England, might there have adjusted the boundary question, and that General Harney might have received instruction from Washington to occupy

---

[48] The Department of Oregon was formed as a direct result of the Indian wars in Washington Territory. Gen. Harney was the first commander of this new command with orders to suppress the Indians of the region. Upon his arrival he found out that Col. George Wright had defeated the Indians and peace was established with the whites

[49] William Harney had a reputation for being an Indian fighter in the Kansas and Nebraska territories. He became the first general, on either side, to be captured during the Civil War but was later released

[50] George Pickett would stay in Washington Territory until the start of the Civil War; he also fathered a child, named James, with a Native American woman. He resigned his commission and later led Confederate forces in the charge that bears his name at Gettysburg, PA

the Island. This idea prevented them from taking forcible possession of the Island, and before they had obtained positive information to the contrary, by allowing an equal number of British Marines to occupy the Island, and British subjects to obtain protection by application to their own magistrates, until proper authorities had mutually agreed to a boundary line and the ownership of the Island.

The news of British preparations for hostilities soon reached Fort Steilacoom, and the steamer *Massachusetts* being then in port, awaiting orders, the Lieutenant Colonel Commanding the District, immediately dispatched me with my company (and a small detachment of infantry, for the protection of Mr. Campbell, the United States Boundary Commissioner at Semiahmoo, against depredations of Northern Indians) with instructions to advise Captain Pickett and, if he required aid, to land my forces and assume command: to observe the proceedings of the British Navy, and to keep Headquarters of the District advised of important occurrences: but the ostensible reason, for appearing in the archipelago, was orders to search for Northern Indians, and remove them beyond our frontier. I reached the harbor on the 1st of August and found Her Majesty's steam-corvette *Tribune* at anchor, and soon after the *Satellite* and *Plumper* arrived with a strong force of British marines and sappers and miners, on board, from Fraser River. I communicated my instructions to Captain Pickett, and awaited coming events. The British officers questioned me closely, about the news by the mail and of Solferino, and they gradually quieted down, so that I felt at liberty to scout for Northern Indians. As soon as General Harney heard of the British preparations, he sent all his available force on the Columbia River over, and directed Lieut. Col. Casey to take them, and his command at Fort Steilacoom, to the support of Captain Pickett. I was soon after ordered ashore to assist in fortifying the Island, but the arrival of General Scott broke up the camp, without completing the defenses. [51]

---

[51] The reasons for the San Juan Island dispute, or as it is also known as the "Pig War", is beyond the scope of this book. Basically, the treaty that established the 49th north parallel as the border between the US and Canada left the ownership of the San Juan Islands in doubt. Gen. Harney wanted to force the issue even to the point of probably starting a war. For this he was relieved of command of the District of Oregon and was forced to turn over the command to Col. George Wright. The issues of ownership were given to the King of Prussia who decided, in 1871, that it was American territory. Haller wrote a short paper called *San Juan and Secession: Possible relation to the War of the Rebellion- Did General Harney try to make trouble with English to aid the Conpiracy? A careful Review of his orders and the*

Fort Mojave

In August, 1859, my company was sent to San Francisco, on arriving there, was ordered to Fort Mojave, on the Colorado River, in New Mexico, over three hundred miles from San Pedro, in California, from whence all our supplies were hauled overland in wagons. This post has been regarded as the very worst in the United States. In the midst of an arid desert, extending a hundred miles to the east and west, located on a barren mesa, overlooking the bottom-lands, there was nothing in common with the familiar scenes we met with everywhere else, but the Cottonwood trees on the river bank, and a garden requiring constant irrigation. The heat of summer is most intense, and wind storms charged with heated sand and dust sweep over the spot for days together. No attempt had been made before my arrival to raise potatoes, or cabbages, and we obtained these, grapes, and other fruit, from Los Angeles, in wagons—a distance of two hundred and eighty-five miles.

While at this post, the United States Astronomical party made their observations to determine the longitude of the point where the 35th parallel of north latitude touched the Colorado River, a short distance below the fort. During their stay the Secession movement was inaugurated. Mr. Mowry, the US Boundary Commissioner, had sent to the fort a large number of young gentlemen, who favored the movement and discussed the matter freely, and, in their letters to the newspapers of San Francisco, giving the *on dits* of Fort Mojave, they made repeated mention of my devotion and attachment to the Union "under all circumstances," as they expressed it.

In 1861, Brig, Gen. Sumner assumed command of the Department of California, when he ordered Fort Mojave to be evacuated, directing me to send the property and the company of the 6th Infantry to Los Angeles, and to proceed to San Diego with my company over land, making the march over four hundred miles. I reached San Diego in June, and the following November embarked my company for New York, and thence proceeded to Washington City, and arrived there on the 19th of December, 1861.

---

circumstances attending the disputed possessions during the year 1859. Haller's theory of the dispute was later discredited by historians.

CIVIL WAR EVENTS

HEADQUARTERS DEPARTMENT OF THE PACIFIC
San Francisco, May 30, 1861

Bvt. Maj. G. O. HALLER,
Captain, Fourth Infantry, Commanding, San Diego, Cal.:

SIR: Orders have been given for sending to you two 24-pounder guns, and the department commander directs that you place them judiciously in battery so as to control as much as possible the harbor at San Diego and at the same time strengthen your position. They will reach you probably on the 3d proximo.

Very respectfully, your obedient servant,

D. C. BUELL,
Assistant Adjutant-General

HEADQUARTERS,
New San Diego Barracks, Cal., June 18, 1861.

Maj. D.C. BUELL,
Assistant Adjutant-General, U. S. Army,
Hdqrs. Department of the Pacific, San Francisco, Cal.:

SIR: I have the honor to report my arrival at this post yesterday with I Company, Fourth Infantry, having a total of fifty-two enlisted men, aggregate fifty-three, being twenty-one days out from Fort Mojave, N. Mex, and having marched in eighteen days 387 miles. I have this day assumed command of this post, and relieved Brevet Major Armistead and his company (F, Sixth Infantry) from duty at this place.

I have the honor to be, very respectfully, your obedient servant,

G. O. HALLER,
Captain, Fourth Infantry, and Brevet Major, Commanding Post

OFFICE U. S. ATTORNEY,

SOUTHERN DIST. OF CALIFORNIA, Los Angeles, August 8, 1861.

General E. V. SUMNER,
Commanding, &c. :

SIR: Doctor Haywood has just shown me some papers written by one Boyd, deceased, containing charges against Lieutenant Haller, of which he has written to you, The documents contain nothing against the loyalty of Lieutenant Haller, only charging him of some small peculations for his private purse. The papers might be of service should the lieutenant prove untrue. I am informed that an expedition is being organized to leave here for Arizona or Sonora under Col. Jack Hays. About three weeks past a Mr. Brown, formerly police officer in Sacramento City, came to this place through Mariposa and Tulare Counties. After a week here he went to San Bernardino and to Holcomb Valley mine, and there holding several meetings secretly with the faithful to Dixie. A Mr. Kelsey, lately from Sonoma, and Major Rollins are to be officers, who are now in San Bernardino. I am informed that about 100 men are enrolled by them. Brown came back here about one week past, and will be up to San Francisco on the next steamer. Of the extent of Jack Hays' movements I am not informed. I shall keep myself informed of the movement here through their confidants, and will inform you of what may occur in their secret meetings. Captain Hancock can inform you more particularly in reference to matters here than I can write. Secessionists are getting more noisy here. We may have to fight them yet. Every county officer is with them. We shall make a strong effort to overthrow them at the election. Union men and Republicans are all united upon one county ticket. We very much regret the removal of Captain Hancock. We regard him as one of the substantial men of the Army, and know he will be right.

Respectfully, your obedient servant,

K. H. DIMMICK

HDQRS. DETACH. 1ST REGT. INFTY. CALIFORNIA VOLS.,
Camp Wright Warners Ranch, San Diego County,
Southern California, November 17, 1861.

Col. JAMES H. CARLETON,
First California Volunteers, Commanding :

COLONEL: Your letter of the 9th containing instructions in reference to Colonel Andrews' command was received this morning too late for me to act. I had already given him transportation for his command, and I suppose by this time he has arrived at Los Angeles in person. The train arrived here just in time for him to get it without any delay, and to-day they are all in San Diego. I followed your instructions and discharged Banning's and Kitchen's train at once. Your letter received today instructed me to take that train and move to Oak Grove or Temecula, but too late--they had gone. I sent on a messenger to Oak Grove, where I knew they would encamp the first night, and requested Mr. Sanford to return here this morning in time to make the return trip, thus not losing time, not feeling authorized, under your positive orders to discharge them at this point, to order or employ them. Mr. Sanford wrote to me that he would very much like to accommodate me and my command, but that his teams could not do it; his animals were worn out; and although he would like to accommodate me without extra charge, but under the circumstances it could not be done. I finally concluded to employ him for one day, and sent Lieutenant Wellman with a proposition to that effect, but on his arrival at Oak Grove the train had gone, and as my instructions to him were not to follow unless he (Sanford) was but a short distance on the road from that point, I have missed the transportation and disarranged your plans, but from no fault of mine, as I conceive. Your orders not to employ, or rather to discharge, their train upon their arrival here, were positive, but the whole cause is the delay of your messenger. He has been nearly five days on the road, and reports having broken down several horses. Your calculation as to the time of arrival here of Colonel Andrews' command was exact, and twenty-four hours earlier arrival of the express would have found the train here, and our camp would now have been at Oak Grove, just where I want to be at this particular time if the information is correct which I have received from your informant. I will now have to remain here until our own train returns, which will not be before the 20th and perhaps not before the 23d, as it has been raining in torrents for several days. To day we have had a specimen of the climate on this ranch. While I am writing (9.40 p.m.) the rain is falling in torrents and the wind is whistling through the camp. If we have any tents standing in the morning I will consider ourselves fortunate. It will depend altogether upon the peg ropes and guys. It was reported to me to-day that the messenger stopped, unsaddled, and remained at Oak Grove for three hours. He must have pursued the same course at other places on the route. The horse he brought in here was entirely broken down, and I had to furnish him with another to proceed to Yuma. Your communication of the 15th instant came in this morning early, and as Colonel Andrews' command has gone on and you have been notified of it I will send him (expressman) back in the morning to Los Angeles. My officers are very busy getting their returns in shape, but without proper blanks it will be difficult for them to have them perfect. I forwarded the post returns to your headquarters a few days since, as well as our weekly return. For several days I had not paper enough in camp to make one out on, and finally had to consolidate. I had sent to Lieutenant Thompson, acting assistant quartermaster, San Diego, several times for some stationery, but he would not send it. I think from the reports of Acting Assistant Quartermaster Vestal, Wagon-master Peale, and Sergeant Wheeling, both he and Captain Roberts were anything but courteous. Major Haller sent me some, which arrived to-day by the ambulance from San Diego. Colonel West sent on the post ambulance with Mrs. Captain Dryer, and as I had no mules for our own I sent it on the San Diego ambulance with her, and by instructions from him will keep it here until I hear from him. I intend to send to Oak Grove a lookout for my friend, Mr. Showalter, and will stop him if I can catch him, or anyone else whom I know to be as deeply dyed a traitor as he is. He has not the excuse that some others have of being born and educated in the South. He is a Pennsylvanian, and never lived in a Southern State in his life, and could have no sympathies of a family nature to excuse him, and I want to see him and a few more. If the party is as large as your informant thinks it is we may have an opportunity to expend some extra cartridges. I have an Indian prisoner here that I would like to have some disposition made of or receive some instructions in regard to him. He has killed several Indians lately, and the chiefs in council decided to hand him over to me for safe-keeping until they could hear from the superintendent of Indian affairs. I addressed a letter to Mr. Baker, supervisor of Indian affairs for the southern district, located at Los Angeles, but have not heard from him. I would like to know from you what disposition to make of him. The Indians have heretofore tried their own people, but they have learned that they have a new chief, and respectfully submit the case to him. At all events, I would like to be advised whether I should hand him back to his people for trial, or what to do with him. I was interrupted by a cry, "The hospital tent is down!" and found it partially true. By lashing and tying it was kept from coming down. We have had a stormy night of it. The guard tents have blown down. Officers' tents, kitchen tents, tent in which I had the ammunition, and a number of others were laid to the ground. It was a gale, and the rain came down in torrents. I think that I have never seen it rain harder. Our tents were all full of water. The men were cheerful and worked hard all night. The morning broke with but little change, excepting it did not rain so hard. The hills all around us are covered with snow. Ice was formed on our tents and ropes. We have had really a specimen of the weather I had reason to expect. I cannot get away from here until our train comes up. We managed to keep our sick from the weather by using all the blankets we could find, the men cheerfully going without themselves. As they were out all night and wet they had no use for them. It continues raining and hailing, but with less wind. We are preparing for another stormy night. It is impossible for the company officers to have all the returns ready that you require by this messenger. Their tents are wet, and writing or ruling is almost out of the question. I have directed them to forward to you letters of explanation. I hope this storm will blow over soon, or we will be in a bad fix. I called your attention in a former letter to you to Jones, of Company D, against whom charges were preferred by Lieutenant Martin.

    Very respectfully, your obedient servant,

EDWIN A. RIGG

COLORADO FERRY, March 4, 1862

Maj. EDWIN A. RIGG
First Infantry California Vols., Comdg. Fort Yuma, Cal.:

DEAR SIR: In answer to your inquiries of yesterday I beg leave to submit the following: I was stationed at Fort Mojave, N. Mex., in the employment of the Government as post interpreter from the 19th of April, 1859, until the 27th of May, 1861, when the post was abandoned, and during that time I had ample opportunities for satisfying myself of the practicability of the route of the thirty-fifth parallel, as it is called. The road from Los Angeles to Fort Mojave as far as Lane's ranch, on the Mojave River, is tolerably good for wagons, being over a rolling country, hard and gravelly. There is plenty of water and tolerable grazing. From Lane's on to Fort Mojave it is over a sandy desert, very scarce of water and destitute of grass. The price of freight paid by the sutler at Fort Mojave was never less than 15 cents per pound, and Government paid Banning, of Los Angeles, as high as 53 cents per pound for freight delivered at the post; distance 285 miles. This fact speaks for itself. From Fort Mojave to Albuquerque, N. Mex., 550 miles, the route was pronounced impracticable by every one who has ever traveled over it, except Mr. Beale. Lieut. J. C. Ives, astronomer to the boundary survey, told me that the route was impracticable for various reasons. First, on account of the very high mountains that you are compelled to cross, and second, on account of the scarcity of water, and that he did not consider it practicable for pack trains more than three months in the year, March, April, and May. Then there was plenty of grass and water. The mail party who were carrying the mail from Saint Joseph, in Missouri, to Stockton, Cal., over this route in the winter and spring of 1859, pronounced it impracticable for wagons. They never made a single trip during the time they were running within schedule time. In company with Maj. G. O. Hailer, U. S. Army, then commanding officer at Fort Mojave, I went out on the route about forty miles over the first chain of mountains east of Fort Mojave and he examined the road to see if it was really as bad as had been represented. He pronounced it impracticable for empty wagons even to be hauled over it. We were compelled to return on account of not being able to haul a lightly loaded Government wagon containing forage for nine animals, blankets and provisions for thirteen men for ten days, in all not more than 1,500 pounds. It was more than we could do to ride over the mountain, but had to dismount and lead. For the truth and correctness of the above statement I beg leave to refer to Major Haller, Fourth Infantry, U.S. Army. Any route north of Fort Mojave and east from Las Vegas is utterly impracticable, and pronounced by every one who has ever seen it the roughest country on the continent. Miners from Potosi, in New Mexico, have found it impossible to penetrate any distance east from the Colorado River. In company with Major Haller, Capt. George A. Johnson, of Fort Yuma, and others, we visited that country last April, and every one came to the conclusion that it is impossible to travel through it. How far north this rough and broken country extends I don't know, but trappers and Indians say for some distance above the forks of the Green and Grand Rivers. In fact, until you arrive at the old Spanish trail at Los Angeles to Albuquerque, N. Mex. This is my unprejudiced opinion in regard to any route near the thirty-fifth parallel or north of it. In regard to the object of my journey to Fort Yuma at present I beg leave to state that I have come here for the purpose of procuring some tools to repair a flouring mill in the town of Oquito, district of Altar, Sonora, where I am at present engaged in the flour trade, and in the event of Government giving protection to loyal American citizens in Arizona I should again take up my residence in that Territory.

 I have the honor to remain, very respectfully, your obedient servant,

P. R. BRADY

Extract from Maj. Gen. George B. McClellan's report of the operations of the Army of the Potomac from July 27, 1861, to November 9, 1862. When the war began Haller moved to New York in order to join up with Gen. McClellan. At the end of McClellan's campaign's in Virginia and Maryland Haller was presented with a sword as a token of appreciation for his service, as commanders of the headquarters guard of the Army of the

Potomac, by the officers of the 93rd New York Infantry.

COMMANDANT OF GENERAL HEADQUARTERS

When the army took the field, for the purpose of securing order and regularity in the camp of headquarters and facilitating its movements, the office of commandant of general headquarters was created, and assigned to Maj. G. O. Haller, Seventh U.S. Infantry. Six companies of infantry were placed under his orders for guard and police duty. Among the orders appended to this report is the one defining his duties, which were always satisfactorily performed.

Orders and reports taken from the Peninsular Campaign

CAMP NEAR ALEXANDRIA,
August 31, 1862--2.30 p.m.

Major Haller is at Fairfax Station with my provost and headquarters guard and other troops. I have requested four more companies to be sent at once and the precautions you direct to be taken.

Under the War Department order of yesterday I have no control over anything except my staff, some 100 men in my camp here, and the few remaining near Fort Monroe. I have no control over the new regiments--- or not know where they are, on anything about them, except those near here. Their commanding officers and those of the works are not under me.

Where I have seen evils existing under my eye, I have corrected them. I think it is the business of General Casey to prepare the new regiments for the field, and a matter between him and General Barnard to order others to the vicinity of Chain Bridge. Neither of them is under my command, and by the War Department order I have no right to give them orders.

GEO. B. McCLELLAN,
Major-General

MCCLELLAN'S HEADQUARTERS,
August 31, 1862.
(Sent through Washington, September 1, 1862, 12.30 a.m.)

Major HALLER Commanding at Fairfax Station:

It is reported that a large force of cavalry and three light batteries of the enemy were this afternoon near Fairfax CourtHouse. They may visit you to-night. Be really for them. Infantry ought to handle cavalry anywhere in such a country as this. Be careful to secure your retreat, and in God's name do not be captured. Keep me constantly posted. If you find your communication with Fairfax CourtHouse irretrievably cut off, destroy the stores and make good your retreat to Alexandria. Communicate the same order to the detachment near you and presumably in your front. If possible fall back by the railroad, retreating only step by step, as you are forced to do so. Don't allow a mere cavalry raid to drive you off. Give ground only- when you are absolutely forced to do so. Communicate by telegraph fully with Colonel Haupt, superintendent of railroads.

By order of General McClellan:
A. V. COLBURN,
Assistant Adjutant-General

SEPTEMBER 1, 1862.

J. H. DEVEREUX:

General Halleck thinks it best not to send forward trains tonight. Those sent can be held at Burke's. I do not apprehend any attack on Fairfax Station to-night, as it is fully covered by very large forces at Fairfax Court-House. Excepting a few empty cars for the wounded, you can withdraw all cars and engines to a safe distance in the rear. Please communicate this information to Major Haller and to McCrickett. We have no intelligence in addition to your own.

H. HAUPT

FAIRFAX, VA., September 1, 1862.

General R. B. MARCY:

I have ridden to and beyond Fairfax Court-House this afternoon to inform myself of our positions and of the enemy, as I have no mounted orderlies to bring in reliable information. I found the right wing of the United States forces approaching Fairfax Court-House. General Hatch posted his brigade in the rifle pits near town, and General Couch's division was but a short distance in his front, toward Centreville. Other troops were going into positions around that place. I was informed the enemy was turning our right flank— -Jackson's corps, consisting of 20,000. While there a cannonade was going on near the turnpike road, say 3 miles from Fairfax Court-House, and when at this camp we heard musketry firing very distinctly, which lasted some time. Results are not known. We are here comfortably safe.

Respectfully,

G. O. HALLER,
Major, Seventh Infantry

Colonel HAUPT, Alexandria:

    The enemy have made a movement to our right, which has thrown our right wing back to Fairfax Court-House. General Couch's division is beyond. General Hatch is at Fairfax Court-House. I saw these generals in position. I hear of the position of others. Teamsters are stampeding. The shower will injure the roads. I think it better to defer sending, until I can give further information, either ordnance or stores, unless particular kinds have been called for.

G. O. HALLER,
Major, Seventh Infantry

FAIRFAX, September 1, 1862— 9 p.m.

Brig. Gen. S. WILLIAMS, Assistant Adjutant-General:

GENERAL: 1st. Your dispatch received. There are now here, exclusive of my command, fully 1,000 troops, organized volunteers, besides a number of fugitives. I consider the number ample to protect this camp, but I fear the volunteers are much demoralized and ready to stampede, or I would have asked to be recalled. There is a colonel here, and all that remains of three regiments of General McDowell's corps, and yet I have had to command and arrange matters.

2d. No one has been assigned to command here. No one sends me orders; all obey me as a military necessity. I have assumed command to secure order. I can give up the command when the general desires me to withdraw without, I believe, violating any rule of service.

3d. The enemy this afternoon turned our right flank and has brought our right wing back to Fairfax Court-House. This wing is in supporting distance in the event of a serious attack from the direction of the Accokeek Creek.

4th. The camp is advantageously located to resist a cavalry raid or light artillery.

5th. Can I march away from this point to the sound of the enemy's guns? There was very heavy firing near to, but on the right of, Centreville this evening. The result is not known. Respectfully,

G. O. HALLER,
Major, Seventh Infantry, Commanding

Col. A. V. COLBURN:

Your dispatch, directing that a portion of Pleasonton's command be sent to Fairfax Court-House, has been received, and the necessary instructions have been given. Your dispatch in relation to the command of Major Haller has also been received, and will be promptly communicated to that officer.

S. WILLIAMS,
Assistant Adjutant General

FAIRFAX, VA., September 2, 1862.

Brigadier-General MARCY, Chief of Staff :

GENERAL: One of our pickets has come in and reports cavalry of the enemy halting near them. We are ready for the raid. Darkness prevents us from seeing their number. They are on the road from the Accotink Creek. We were joined by some of Banks' troops in the night, but the colonel of them is going to have his own way, and is unwilling to assist as I have proposed. He is really in our way if he does not move.

Respectfully,

G. O. HALLER,
Major, Seventh Infantry

Orders and reports taken from the Gettysburg Campaign. At this time Haller was in Pennsylvania and volunteered his services to Gen. Couch, commander of the Department of Susquehanna, and joined his staff as an aide-de-camp with orders to take charge of military operations and volunteers in the York area. He was also responsible for burning a bridge across the Susquehanna River to deny Confederate troops easy access to Philadelphia, organizing and placement of artillery and troops around the Harrisburg area. During the last few days of June he was setting up roadblocks against the advancing Confederate forces moving towards Gettysburg.

HARRISBURG, PA.,
June 22, 1863,.

Major-General SCHENCK, Baltimore:

Nothing new this morning. Will keep you informed. Major Haller is my aide at Gettysburg.

D. N. COUCH,
Major-General

HARRISBURG, PA., June 25, 1863.
(Received 8.10 p.m.)

General H. W. HALLECK,
General-in-Chief:

    I have nothing reliable as to rebel infantry in the Valley to-day. Their cavalry advance is within 5 miles of Carlisle. Haller at Gettysburg, with some cavalry and a regiment of infantry. Only know that the rebels are in the mountains. They are also making cavalry raids in Pennsylvania north of Hancock. Most of the men that rushed to arms at Altoona and south are rushing home.

D. N. COUCH

YORK, June 27, 1863.

Major-General COUCH:

    Off toward Wrightsville and Columbia. The enemy approaching with the Gettysburg force, about 4,000. Will respect private property if not resisted, and borough authorities wish no resistance.

G. O. HALLER,
Major Seventh Infantry, and Aide-de-Camp

HEADQUARTERS DEPARTMENT OF THE SUSQUEHANNA,
June 28, 1863.

Colonel FRICK,
Commanding, Columbia:

    York has surrendered. Our troops will fall back from there to Wrightsville to-night.
    If Major Haller is with them, he is my aide-de-camp.
    Have reliable men sent down to the Conowingo Bridge. Impress horses, and send good officers or volunteers.
    The commanding officer will take up planks, and in no event should that bridge fall into enemy's hands, or any fords.
    Tell the people of Lancaster that the time has come for action. Have all boats and rafts along the river brought on this side.

D. N. COUCH,
Major-General

Columbia, June 29, 1863.

Maj. O. O. HALLER,
Commanding District of the Susquehanna:

Having received orders from you to employ a force of carpenters and bridge-builders for the purpose of cutting and throwing a span of the Columbia Bridge, crossing the Susquehanna, between the boroughs of Columbia and Wrightsville, I engaged such a force for that purpose.

Guards were placed upon the bridge during the afternoon and night of Saturday, the 27th instant, up to half past 7 o'clock of Sunday evening, the 28th instant, when, the bridge having been weakened at two points, one of which was the fourth span from Wrightsville (there being twenty-eight spans, and the structure a mile and a quarter in length), by the removal of all excepting the arches and a very small portion of the lower chords, the arches were bored and loaded with powder, with fuses attached, all ready to apply the match.

At a given signal by your aide, Maj. C. McL. Knox, in the presence of and by approval of Colonel Frick, at about 7.30 o'clock, all the forces having passed over from the borough of Wrightsville, the plank flooring was removed and the match applied to the fuse by John Q. Denny, John Lockhard, Jacob Rich, and Jacob Miller, persons stationed for this purpose. Every charge was perfect and effective.

The rebel cavalry and artillery approaching the bridge at the Wrightsville end, Colonel Frick, in order to more effectually destroy the connection (the bridge not falling), ordered it to be fired, at which time the rebel artillery were playing upon us.

The following gentlemen--E. K. Smith, esq., civil engineer; William Fasick, Isaac Ruel, Henry Burgen, John Gilbert, Fred Bush, A. P. Moore, George W. Green, Michael Luphart, John B. Bachman, Davis Murphy, Westly Up, Michael Shuman, Henry Duck, and S. W. Finney, who assisted me in this responsible and dangerous work--will please receive my own as well as the most heartfelt thanks of the community, for effecting the object that prevented the rebels from crossing the Susquehanna at this point.

With high regard, I remain, your humble servant,
ROBERT CRANE

HEADQUARTERS DEFENSES OF LANCASTER COUNTY,
Columbia, Pa., July 1, 1863.

CAPTAIN[52]: I have the honor to report that, in compliance with General Orders, No. 14, from the Department of the Susquehanna, I left Harrisburg on the morning of the 24th ultimo, and arrived here on the afternoon of the same day, and immediately sent four companies, in command of Lieutenant-Colonel Green, over the river.

On the morning of the 25th ultimo, I sent four more companies to that officer, with instructions to take up a position near the York turnpike, about a half mile from Wrightsville.

Hearing, on the afternoon of the 27th, that the enemy were in the vicinity of York, I ordered my two remaining companies to report to Lieutenant-Colonel Green that we might be prepared to resist any sudden attempt by the enemy to get possession of the bridge at this point.

Late in the evening of the same day, I crossed the river, assumed command, and disposed my force for defense.

During the night, our force was increased by four companies from Columbia (three white and one colored), numbering about 175 men.

Very early next morning, having obtained intrenching tools from citizens of Columbia and the Pennsylvania Railroad Company, my own men and the negro company (the other three companies from Columbia having left for their homes) dug rifle-pits on either side of the turnpike.

During the morning, a detachment of convalescent soldiers from York, and the Patapsco Guards, in all about 250 men, joined me, and they were posted on the left of the town, protecting the left flank of my position. They were placed under command of Lieutenant-Colonel Green. We were also joined by scattered fragments of the Twentieth Regiment Pennsylvania Volunteer Militia, under Lieutenant-Colonel Sickles, during the morning,

---

[52] Addressed to Capt. Robert Le Roy, Asst. Adjt. Gen., Dept. of the Susquehanna

which I posted on the right of the town as a protection to the right flank.

The work of intrenching was continued until the approach and attack of the enemy, about 5.30 p.m., and, while the work was in progress, I selected, with the assistance of Major Haller, aide-de-camp to the commanding general, the several points at which to post my limited number of men.

The main body of the enemy, about 2,500 strong, composed of cavalry, artillery, and infantry, took up their position about 6 p.m. on the turnpike in our immediate front, and within three-quarters of a mile of our rifle-pits. A force of cavalry and infantry moved down the railroad on our left, and attacked our skirmishers, who, after replying to their fire for a short time, retired to the main body, which kept up a steady fire, and held the enemy in check until they received orders to retire to the bridge. The rebels succeeded in getting a battery in position on the elevated ground on our right and a section in our immediate front. These guns were used most vigorously against those of my command occupying the rifle-pits.

In the meantime, they sent a column of infantry, under cover of a high hill on our right, within a few hundred yards of the river. None but their skirmishers approached within range of the guns of the men occupying the rifle-pits, and these being in a grain-field, and obscured from our view, excepting when they would rise to fire, it was difficult to do then much harm or dislodge them. They depended exclusively upon their artillery to drive us from our position here. Having no artillery ourselves on that side of the river with which to reply, and after retaining our position for about one and a quarter hours, and discovering that our remaining longer would enable the enemy to reach the river on both of my flanks, which I was unable to prevent because of the small number of men under my command, and thus get possession of the bridge, cut off our retreat, and secure a crossing of the Susquehanna, which I was instructed to prevent, I retired in good order, and crossed the bridge to the Lancaster side.

Before the enemy had left York for the river here, I made, as I supposed, every necessary arrangement to blow up one span of the Columbia Bridge. When they got within sight, the gentlemen charged with the execution of that work repaired promptly to the bridge, and commenced sawing off the arches and heavy timbers preparatory to blowing it up with powder, which they had arranged for that purpose. After an abundance of time was allowed, and after I supposed every man of my command was over the river, and when the enemy had entered the town with his artillery, and reached the barricade at the bridge-head, I gave the order to light the fuse. The explosion took place, but our object in blowing up the bridge failed. It was then that I felt it to be my duty, in order to prevent the enemy from crossing the river and marching on to Harrisburg in the rear, destroying on his route railroads and bridges, to order the bridge to be set on fire. The bridge was completely destroyed, though a vigorous attempt was made to save a part by the soldiers.

I was materially assisted in my operations by Captain Strickler, who had charge of a small force of cavalry, acting as scouts. I feel indebted to him for much reliable information as to the movements and force of the enemy.

Major [Charles C.] Haldeman, formerly of the Twenty-third Regiment Pennsylvania Volunteers, volunteered his services, and rendered me very efficient aid.

Lieutenant-Colonel [David B.] Green, who had charge of the left flank of the position, with a force of 250 men, and Major [George L.] Fried, who took charge of the left wing of the Twenty-seventh Regiment Pennsylvania Volunteer Militia, behaved with accustomed coolness and gallantry, and brought off their forces in most excellent order.

Great praise is due to Captain [Joseph] Oliver, Company D, Twenty-seventh Pennsylvania Volunteer Militia, commanding a body of skirmishers of about 70 men, for the skillfulness and boldness with which he handled his men. The officers and men of my command generally did their whole duty.

Before closing this report, justice compels me to make mention of the excellent conduct of the company of negroes from Columbia. After working industriously in the rifle-pits all day, when the fight commenced they took their guns and stood up to their work bravely.

They fell back only when ordered to do so.

I herewith inclose a list of casualties.

The prisoners taken--18 in number--were all from the Twentieth Pennsylvania Volunteer Militia, including Lieutenant-Colonel [William H.] Sickles, of that regiment. From information received since the engagement, I feel convinced that if my orders had been promptly obeyed, no prisoners would have been taken.

I have the honor to be, very respectfully, your obedient servant,

JACOB G. FRICK,
Colonel, Commanding

HEADQUARTERS DEPARTMENT OF THE SUSQUEHANNA,
Chambersburg, Pa., July 15, 1863.

SIR[53]: In obedience to instructions from the honorable Secretary of War, I left Washington June 11, for Harrisburg, in order to assume command of the newly organized Department of the Susquehanna.

After an interview with His Excellency Governor Curtin and gentlemen of his council, an order was prepared and issued to the department, calling for a corps of troops for State defense. This was in accordance with instructions received from Mr. Stanton.

The Governor also issued a proclamation to the people of the State in connection with my order.

On the 15th, 800 of the enemy's mounted force appeared at Chambersburg, 16 miles north of the Maryland line. They were closely watched by about 120 men of the First New York Cavalry, under Captain Boyd, who covered the wagon train of General Milroy on its retreat from Winchester, Va., toward Harrisburg, Pa.

At this date there were not 250 organized men in the department for duty. The sick in the hospital at York were removed, as well as the United States stores at Carlisle.

Lieutenant-Colonel Coppee, of Philadelphia, volunteered his services to the State, and was sent to Altoona to arrange with the officers of the Pennsylvania Railroad Company for the defense of that point, the bridges crossing the Juniata, as well as the mountain passes, southerly toward Bedford, McConnellsburg, and London. Comparatively few troops offered for State defense.

The President called for volunteers for six-months' service, and Governor Curtin issued his proclamation for 50,000 men. This was on the 15th, and men in masses began to assemble at Philadelphia, Harrisburg, Huntingdon, Altoona, &c.

---

[53] Report of Maj. Gen. Darius N. Couch, commanding Department of the Susquehanna

The militia of Pennsylvania was not organized. Farmers in the threatened parts were directed to remove their stock.

On the 17th, the only company of infantry, Captain McGowan's, from York Hospital, was sent to Shippensburg. Rebel advance fell back on the 18th to Greencastle. Some 2,500 of General Milroy's force, in retreating, via Hancock, arrived' near Bedford Springs, where their commander joined them. They were a good deal demoralized. Colonel Higgins re-enforced Milroy with 1,200 men, without blankets or camp equipage. Militia regiments from New York began to arrive. New Jersey sent one regiment for three days. Other companies from that State reported at Harrisburg.

The Secretary of War placed the arsenals and clothing depots at my disposal; also gave me ample authority to receive, subsist, and arm whatever troops might be offered from the neighboring States.

The New York militia were mustered into the United States service for thirty days. The Pennsylvanians generally declined to be mustered for six months. Finally, a portion consented to serve during "the existence of the emergency."

The heights on the right bank of the Susquehanna, opposite to Harrisburg, were being fortified, in order to cover that city and the important bridges. Some of the patriotic citizens of that city volunteered to work in the trenches; others were paid. The colored population were not behind their white brethren in giving assistance.

The Eighth and Seventy-first New York Militia went to Chambersburg on the 19th.

Rebel advance of infantry and artillery, 8,000 men, reported at Hagerstown.

Brig. Gen. W. F. Smith joined after returning from Altoona and Bedford. He was placed in command of all the troops and defenses opposite Harrisburg. The works were being pushed under the chief engineer of the department, Capt. J. B. Wheeler, assisted by Maj. James Brady, First Pennsylvania Artillery; Captain Wilson, of the Pennsylvania Railroad, and other employes of that and the Northern Central road.

Every effort was made to organize artillery and get it into position. Major [Granville O.] Haller, acting aide-de-camp, was sent to Gettysburg to take command.

Capt. David McConaughy, of Gettysburg, in company with others, were sent out as scouts to gain information.

Colonel Thomas, Twentieth Pennsylvania Volunteers, had the defense of the bridges of the Northern Central Railroad.

On the evening of the 22d, the rebel cavalry advanced upon Chambersburg, followed by heavy masses of infantry and artillery. It was the head of their army, under General Lee. A part of Ewell's corps advanced toward Carlisle, which place they occupied on the 27th and 28th by 12,000 men, our forces, under Brigadier-General Knipe, falling back to near Harrisburg. The remainder of Ewell's corps, 8,000, crossed from Chambersburg to Gettysburg on the 26th; drove in our scouts with their supports, with a loss to us of 176 men missing and prisoners of the Twenty-sixth Emergency Regiment. From that place the enemy moved in the direction of York.

The chief burgess and a deputation of citizens met this force 9 miles from the town, and formally surrendered. It was occupied by General Early on the 28th. A body of 2,500 of the rebels immediately pushed toward Columbia, drove in the troops at Wrightsville, under Colonel Frick, who retreated across the river and burned the bridge. Same day, their advance approached to within 3 miles of Harrisburg, engaging our pickets and reconnoitered the works.

Colonel Thomas, Twentieth Regiment, in charge of bridges near York, retired toward the Susquehanna.

The call of June 15 brought only seven full regiments. The Governor obtained the sanction of the President, and called out 60,000 militia for State service. These rendezvoused at Harrisburg, Reading, and Huntingdon. Up to this time, New York had sent nearly 6,000 men.

Col. E. Franklin, a citizen of Lancaster, had been placed in command of the fords and bridges on the Lower Susquehanna, to Conowingo, in Maryland, some of which were guarded by citizens partially armed with shot-guns.

Five thousand men of the counties bordering on the Juniata filled the passes leading to their homes, and threw up military works. They were an army of bushwhackers, commanded by ex-officers.

Brigadier-General Smith advanced to Carlisle July 1, with 3,000 men. During the night, Lee's cavalry, 3,200 strong, surrounded the place, and, after demanding its surrender, shelled the town, retiring before the next morning in the direction of Gettysburg, where General Lee was hastily concentrating, having been forced to this by the rapid movements of the Army of the Potomac, under General Meade.

The battle of Gettysburg was fought on July 1, 2, and 3, when the rebels commenced falling back to Hagerstown. Brigadier-General Knipe joining Smith, the latter moved in the direction of Gettysburg through the mountains, via Pine Grove, in order to make a diversion in favor of Meade by attacking Lee's flank and rear. This movement compelled the latter to keep a large force in line of battle near Cashtown. Smith was ordered by General Meade to join him at Gettysburg. Subsequently it was countermanded, and he followed the retreating army of Lee, via Altodale, to the vicinity of Waynesborough, where he effected a junction with one of Meade's brigades, under Brigadier-General Neill. Smith's division was mostly composed of New York troops, including one brigade of Pennsylvania emergency men, under Colonel Brisbane, acting brigadier-general. I respectfully refer to the elaborate report of Brigadier-General Smith.

Major-General Sigel was assigned to duty in this department, and took command of the rendezvous at Reading. Major-General Stahel was present as chief of cavalry.

Major-General Dana, on duty at Philadelphia, reported to me at Chambersburg on the 11th, and was assigned to the command of the Second Division, composed of Pennsylvania militia, excepting two New York regiments, under the command of Brigadier-General Yates.

Colonels Beaver and Miles, both of the Second Army Corps, dangerously wounded at Chancellorsville, commanded Camps Curtin and Huntingdon.

Colonel Pierce, Twelfth Pennsylvania Cavalry, who had succeeded Milroy, killed, wounded, and captured a company of rebel cavalry at McConnellsburg.

On July 5, Captain Jones, First New York Cavalry, attacked Lee's wagon train near Greencastle, and brought off 645 prisoners, 300 of whom were wounded, 90 wagons, and 1 piece of artillery.

Had Colonel Pierce fully carried out my instructions, he would have inflicted very heavy loss upon the rebels, in breaking up their trains. He sent in nearly 1,000 prisoners; General Smith about 300, with some wagons and horses. This officer joined his force with those of General Meade, the latter having under advisement the breaking up of this division and distributing the regiments among the brigades of his army. This course was recommended to that officer and approved by General Smith. Lee, however, recrossed the Potomac before it was accomplished. Thus ended, disastrously to the enemy, their invasion of Maryland and Pennsylvania.

I received from Governor Curtin and State officers every assistance. Among the latter, more prominently were Col. John A. Wright, aide-de-camp; Hon. William M. Meredith, attorney-general; Adjutant-General [A. L.] Russell, Commissary-General Irwin, General Cameron, Col. T. A. Scott, Judge Watts, Hon. Charles McAllister, Colonel McClure, Judge [Francis M.] Kimmell, Colonel Stumbaugh, and J. N. Du Barry, together with a very great number of gentlemen residing within the limits of the department, who lent their assistance in working for the common cause.

The Governor of New York pushed forward his regiments with alacrity. They were generally armed and equipped ready for field service, and their arrival brought confidence.

Among the patriotic associations in the country, the Union League, of Philadelphia, is not surpassed for its vigor and efficient labor. It alone placed several regiments in the field.

The militia of Pennsylvania raised to resist the invasion was composed of men from all classes and professions, and was a fine body of men.

My thanks are due to the following-named gentlemen, who freely gave their services to the State, and served as volunteers on my staff; they were stationed in various sections of the department: Lieut. Col. Henry Coppee, military secretary; Majors Wilson and Wayne MacVeagh; Capts. David McConaughy, W. A. H. Lewis, and A. Wright; and Cadets [Reuben W.] Petrikin, [William] Krause, and [Charles W.] Raymond, from West Point, extra aides-de-camp.

New York sent nineteen regiments and one battery, commanded by the following brigadier-generals: Brigadier-Generals Hall, Yates, Ewen, Crooke, and Smith.

Pennsylvania furnished eight regiments of emergency men, twenty-two regiments of three-months' militia, five companies of artillery, one battalion of six-months' infantry, two regiments and one battalion of six-months' cavalry, and one battalion of three-months' cavalry. The three-months' men were generally organized between July 4 and 11 of the same month.

New Jersey sent one battalion of infantry that remained until after the invasion. Number of prisoners reported, 1,341, of whom nearly 500 were taken under arms, 400 wounded, and the remainder stragglers and deserters. This does not include quite a number who escaped through the mountains and went north, being aided in this by the citizens.

I am, sir, very respectfully, your obedient servant,

D. N. COUCH,
Major-General, Commanding

YORK, PA., July 21, 1863.

GENERAL: I have the honor to submit the following details in connection with the defense at the Columbia Bridge:

The troops from York, under my charge, arrived at Wrightsville about 7.30 p.m. A scene presented itself which can hardly be exaggerated. Locomotives, tenders, and cars of all descriptions lined the railroad, awaiting removal to Columbia.

The turnpike road leading to the bridge was lined with large wagons, removing property of citizens across the Susquehanna. There was much time lost by teamsters having to halt and pay toll and the transportation agents not having sufficient animals for the extraordinary demands upon them.

Having obtained quarters for my command and arranged for their suppers, I sought Dr. [Barton] Evans, president of bridge company, and pointed out the detention at the bridge, and, the removal by our people being involuntary, urged that tolls should not be exacted. The president at once threw the bridge open to travel free. I then authorized, in your name the transportation agents to impress teams to remove the rolling stock, when the crossing became exceedingly active. All night long the work went on, and I am happy to say everything was passed over safely excepting one car, which seemed to have been left designedly, as I repeatedly urged its removal.

I sought for Col. J. G. Frick, commanding Twenty-seventh Pennsylvania Militia, whose regiment was guarding the approaches from York, and at a very late hour met him. I found him confident of the courage of his troops, and eager to resist anything like a raid to destroy the bridge, we then arranged to throw up rifle-pits and use every precaution to save the bridge that our forces would enable us to do. He sent at once for intrenching tools, and early next morning the colonel, Maj. C. C. Haldeman, and myself examined the approaches, and traced out the line of rifle-pits and positions for our troops.

To prevent the enemy crossing the Columbia Bridge, I arranged and relied upon the following defenses:

1. Two Napoleon guns and one iron rifle piece, placed in battery in Columbia, to rake the bridge in case the enemy forced it while our troops were relying on other defenses. These guns were manned by a detachment of the Twenty-seventh Pennsylvania Militia, under Lieutenant [Delaplaine J.] Ridgway, and some citizens of Columbia. There was also a small guard of the Twenty-seventh Pennsylvania Militia at the Columbia side of the bridge.

2. The fourth span (from Wrightsville) of the bridge was selected, and mechanics were employed to separate the roof and sides, leaving only "the arches and a very small portion of the lower chords" for crossing over. It was expected that holes bored into these arches and filled with powder would, by exploding the powder, shiver the timber and cause the span, about 200 feet long, to drop into the river, and thus render the bridge useless to the enemy. This work was superintended by Mr. Robert Crane, who had previously, upon the first alarm, begun this work, and who has cheerfully rendered me every assistance. His report is herewith inclosed, marked A. Lieutenant Randall, of the City Troop, first, and subsequently Maj. C. McLean Knox, Ninth New York Cavalry, was placed by the mines to observe whether the enemy approached, with instructions to order the mines to be exploded in time to prevent them from getting over the doomed arch. I relied very much upon the success of this arrangement.

3. A tete-de-pont immediately around the bridge to cover the retreat of our troops. A few hopper cars (iron), loaded with iron ore, were retained to barricade the main street leading from York to the bridge. The side streets were obstructed by boards piled together so as to make complete breastworks for defense. This work was performed by the citizens under the directions of Mr. [Samuel H.] Mann, of Wrightsville, the provost-marshal, to whom I indicated the lines of defense. This bridge-head was garrisoned by about 50 of the Twenty-sixth Pennsylvania Militia, very much worn down by their retreat from Gettysburg, and a small guard at the bridge, of the Twenty-seventh Pennsylvania Militia.

4. About three-fourths of a mile in front of the bridge is a ridge which curves in toward the Susquehanna River, and on the upper side, near the river, beyond this, is another height, both of which are good positions for defense against infantry and cavalry. Two small creeks run at the foot of these eminences. But outside of these, above and below Wrightsville, are ridges making in at right angles to the river which, with artillery, would command these defenses. With the force at 'our command, it was impossible for us to place troops on these ridges. To defend the bridge successfully, these ridges would have to be occupied by our troops, supported by artillery. It would have required, perhaps, five times our number to have garrisoned the line extending from the upper to the lower ridge.

Our defense, therefore, contemplated resistance to a raid by the enemy's cavalry and mounted infantry which might be thrown forward to destroy the bridge. York was not occupied by the enemy until 10 a.m. Sunday, June 28, and it was not known what the enemy's designs were. If they came with a column to invade the county it would be impossible to defend the bridge successfully. We therefore strengthened our position by rifle-pits as far as our supply of tools would permit, determined to hold our ground until the development of the enemy showed a superiority in numbers, aided by cannon.

The extent of Wrightsville and the nature of the ground required a line of defense over 1 mile in length.

To garrison this line we had Col. J. G. Frick's Twenty-seventh Pennsylvania Militia (excluding artillery and bridge guards), 650; York Battalion (invalids and Patapsco Guards), 238; Lieut. Col. William H. Sickles, 3 companies Twentieth Pennsylvania Militia, 200; total, 1,088. These troops were disposed of as follows:

The Twenty-seventh Pennsylvania Militia, Colonel Frick commanding, occupied the rifle-pits in front and on both sides the York turnpike, with one company thrown forward on the pike to picket the road.

The York Battalion (composed of old soldiers, wounded, and convalescents, who have been under fire) was placed under command of Lieutenant-Colonel Green, Twenty-seventh Pennsylvania Militia, and posted on the left of Colonel Frick's regiment, extending to the Susquehanna River, the Patapsco Guards in reserve. This line was most likely to be seriously assailed, as the ground here most favored the enemy's approach.

The battalion of Twentieth Pennsylvania Militia, Lieutenant-Colonel Sickles commanding, guarded the approaches on the right of the Twenty-seventh Pennsylvania Militia to the river.

The Adams County Cavalry were thrown forward on the York pike and neighboring heights to ascertain if the enemy approached, and their probable force. About a dozen were sent forward to observe the Old Baltimore road. The City Troop patrolled Wrightsville, and obliged every soldier to repair to his company. A few of the City Troop were selected as messengers, and stationed with the field officers to carry communications.

My information represented York as having been occupied at 10 a.m. by 1,000 rebels, and our scouts were driven within our lines without having ascertained the enemy's number or that they had artillery. There was reason to hope that their number was not formidable, and we might save the Bridge. However, as the enemy approached, they presented a deployed line of cavalry and infantry skirmishers, which spread to the summit of the ridge on our left, and in the distance a mass of infantry was observed.

The enemy advanced very slowly, feeling their way, and occasionally firing, which our men returned. The luxuriant grain in the fields in our front and the woods on our left covered the assailants, while our rifle-pits protected our men; hence the firing did but little injury.

For casualties I have to request that battalion commanders be called upon for reports.

As the firing began, I received a telegram from Col. William B. Thomas, Twentieth Pennsylvania Militia, at Bainbridge, Pa., which is herewith inclosed (marked B), saying: "A scout just arrived from York reports the enemy advancing on Columbia with three brigades of infantry and one regiment of cavalry. If you," &c. This I deemed it my duty to show to Colonel Frick. The colonel advised retreat, but, dreading confusion when retreating with inexperienced militia, I proposed to the colonel to destroy the span of the Columbia Bridge, thus cutting off all hope of retreat by that route, and hold our ground as long as practicable. We had previously arranged that if cut off from the bridge our retreat should be along the hills bordering the Susquehanna River to some ford above Wrightsville. The colonel, however, was decidedly of the opinion that we could retreat yet without being hard pressed by the enemy. I accordingly sent an order to Lieutenant-Colonel Sickles to withdraw in good order, and then to Lieutenant-Colonel

Green, while Colonel Frick was to fall back as soon as he saw our flanks well drawn in.

I saw the movement commenced in good order; then hastened to the bridge and saw the mines were ready, and found the artillery in position prepared for the worst.

The enemy had selected positions for their cannon, and, as the retreat began, opened upon the men and town, firing some 40 rounds. Our retreat was so unexpected to them, so quietly and simultaneously performed, as to disconcert them.

Our troops defiled from the bridge in good order; the companies were promptly formed in the street and the battalion there reformed. An agreeable slight presented itself as the colors of the Twenty-seventh Pennsylvania Militia, held by a sergeant, followed by the regiment in good order, cheering it, marched last from the bridge.

Having selected camping grounds, through the assistance of Maj. C. C. Haldeman the troops were conducted into camp; details were made to guard the river bank; our cannon were provided with horses by impressment, upon your authority (see orders hereto annexed, marked C), as it was necessary that they should be in readiness to move at a moment s notice. Every precaution was taken to prevent the enemy from crossing to the Lancaster County side.

Our troops reached the bridge in advance of the enemy, and all of our men were passed over until the enemy was seen descending the hill, when the mines were exploded. Colonel Frick, who conducted the retreat at the rear, halted the bridge span to see that the work would be effectually performed.

The explosion unfortunately failed to drop the span into the river, and the enemy's approach required speedy action. Colonel Frick accordingly ordered the bridge to be set on fire, and the seasoned timbers readily took fire, carrying the flames rapidly toward Wrightsville and Columbia.

In Columbia the citizens and soldiers, attracted there by the fire, procured axes and entered the bridge to cut away such parts as would lessen the flames, hoping, by means of the fire-engines, to extinguish the flames before reaching the town, where it would endanger houses. The rapidity of the flames and intense heat defeated all efforts, and the bridge was entirely consumed; also a building near it. The firemen prevented, by their exertions, the spreading of the flames in the town.

In Wrightsville the flames extended to private houses, and the Confederate troops made great exertions to extinguish the fires.

On Monday, June 29, at the request of Colonel Frick, I accompanied him around Columbia on a reconnaissance, and determined the best positions for troops and defenses. This work had just been completed when we received the gratifying intelligence that the enemy had retired from Wrightsville. Soon after I received your telegram directing me to go to Bainbridge at once to see that Colonel Thomas put himself in a position to defend the different fords at every sacrifice, dig pits, make abatis, &c. At 2 p.m. I rode up to Chestnut Riffles, and thence to Bainbridge.

Before concluding, I deem it proper to add that Colonel Frick's conduct throughout was zealous and patriotic, and deserves your highest commendation. Lieutenant-Colonel Green, commanding the York Battalion, Captain [Robert] Bell, of the Adams County Cavalry, and Lieutenant Randall, of the City Troop, faithfully obeyed their orders. Maj. Charles McLean Knox, Ninth New York Cavalry, and Mr. Samuel Young, of Reading, gave me every assistance.

I regret to have to add that the conduct of Colonel Sickles and two companies of the Twentieth Pennsylvania Militia deserves investigation. It has been represented to me that the lieutenant-colonel and some 15 or 20 of his men have unnecessarily, but deliberately, surrendered to the Confederate troops. Some of the men threw away their arms, and the two companies, without authority, hurried away from Columbia, straggling along the road to Lancaster and filling the country with alarming reports.

The Adams County Cavalry, who were scouting the Old Baltimore road, it seems came into Wrightsville while in the hands of the enemy, and tried to cross the bridge, but found it on fire. They then retreated under the fire of the enemy, having 1 horse shot and a soldier wounded by the fall, but he escaped capture by concealing himself in a house. One soldier and horse were captured. The others reached Safe Harbor in safety, and afterward joined their company.

I have the honor to be, general, very respectfully, your obedient servant,

G. O. HALLER,
Major Seventh Infantry, (late) Aide-de-Camp pro tem

CONGRESSIONAL ACTION

After 16 years of trying to clear his name Haller, with help of some influential friends, finally persuaded Congress to order a Court of Inquiry about his dismissal. During this time he and his family lived at Coupeville, Whidbey Island, Washington Territory where he was a successful businessman. The house where he lived while trying to clear his name still stands and is on private land.

IN THE HOUSE OF REPRSENTIVES[54]

December 7, 1877

Read twice, referred to the Committee on military Affairs, and ordered to be printed. February 27, 1878

Reported with an amendment, committed to the Committee of the Whole House, and ordered to be printed.

Mr. Jacobs[55], by unanimous consent, introduced the following joint resolution:

JOINT RESOLUTION

Requiring the assembling of a court of inquiry in the case of Major Granville O. Haller, late of the Seventh Infantry, United States Army.

Resolved by the Senate and House of Representatives of the United States of America in Congress assembled, that the Secretary of War is hereby required to order a military court-martial or court of inquiry to inquire into the matter of the dismissal of Major Granville O. Haller, late of the Seventh Infantry, United States Army; said court to be fully empowered to confirm or annul the action of the War Department by which said Haller was summarily dismissed the service on or about the ninth of July, anno Domini eighteen hundred

---

[54] House Resolution 63, 45th Congress, 2nd Session
[55] Orange Jacobs, Delegate from Washington Territory (which became a State in 1889), 1875-79; mayor of Seattle, WA, 1879-80; member Washington territorial council, 1885-87; superior court judge in Washington, 1896-1900. Died in Seattle, May 21, 1914. Interment at Mt. Pleasant Cemetery, Seattle.

and sixty-three, said court to be assemble at such convenient place as may be designated by the President; and the findings to have the effect of restoring said Haller to his rank, with the promotion to which he would be entitled, if it be found that he was wrongfully dismissed, or to confirm his dismissal, if it be otherwise found. Said Haller shall notify the commanding officer of his readiness to appear before said court; and he shall have reasonable notice of the time of the assembling of the same: Provided, that said Haller shall receive no pay or allowances of any kind whatsoever for the time he was out of the service.

IN THE SENATE OF THE UNITED STATES[56]

February 28, 1879- Ordered to be printed.

Mr. Spencer[57], from the Committee on Military Affairs, submitted the following report: [To accompany joint resolution H. Res. 63]

The Committee on Military Affairs, to whom was referred the joint resolution (H. Res. 63) requiring the assembly of a court of inquiry in the case of Major. Granville O. Haller, later of the Seventh United States Infantry, have had the same under consideration, and submit the following report:

This joint resolution directs a military court of inquiry to be held for the purpose of determining whether this officer was properly and legally dismissed the Army; if yea, then the dismissal to stand; if nay, then the judgment of the court to operate as a revocation of the action by which he was summarily dismissed. The case was reported by General Maish, of the House Committee on Military Affairs, as follows:

[House Report No. 375, Forty-fifth Congress, second session]

Mr. Maish[58], from the Committee on Military Affairs, submitted the following report, to accompany joint resolution H. R. 63:

---

[56] Senate Report 860, 45th Congress, 3rd Session
[57] Sen. George Spencer, Alabama, 1868-79, 1872-. Died in Washington, D.C., February 19, 1893. Interment at Arlington National Cemetery

The Committee on Military Affairs, to whom was referred the joint resolution (H. Res. 63) authorizing a court of inquiry in the case of Granville O. Haller, late of the Seventh Infantry, United States Army, having had the same under consideration, beg leave to submit the following report:

    Granville O. Haller entered the Army as second lieutenant of the Fourth Infantry on the 17th day of November, 1839. In 1840 he joined his regiment at Fort Gibson, and saw active and continuous service in the Florida war acting as adjutant of his regiment.

    In 1845 the Third and Fourth Regiments of Infantry became the "army of occupation" on the borders of Texas, and took possession of Saint Joseph's Island and Corpus Christi. He there acted as brigade major of the Third Brigade—a title now obsolete.

    In 1846 the "army of occupation" marched to the Rio Grande, and encamped opposite Matamoras. He there was appointed commissary of the Third Brigade. Relinquishing that position for one of more active duties in the field, he participated in the battles of Palo Alto, Resaca de la Palma, Vera Cruz, Cerro Gordo, and in all the battles in the valley of Mexico.

    In the terrible battle of El Molino del Rey he was one of the storming party, and was not only complimented by his superior officer for his gallantry, but on the 8th September, 1847, received his commission of captain by brevet for gallant and meritorious conduct in that battle.

    On the 13th of September, 1847, he was commissioned major by brevet for gallant and meritorious conduct in the battle of Chapultepec.

    In 1852 Major Haller and his company were sent to the Pacific coast, and in 1853 was stationed at Fort Dalles, in the then Territory of Oregon. He actively participated in the Oregon Indian war of 1855 and 1856, and at or near the Yakima River, in Washington Territory, was surrounded by a vastly superior force of hostile Indians, fought for three days, and finally cut his way out, losing over a third of his command.

    In 1859 Major Haller and his company were ordered to Fort Mojave, on the Colorado River, New Mexico.

---

[58] Rep. Levi Maish, Pennsylvania, 1875-79, 1887-91. Died in 1899. Interment at Arlington National Cemetery

In 1861 he was ordered to this city[59]. Upon his arrival he found he had been promoted to the rank of major, was assigned to Brig. Gen. Andrew Porter's[60] staff, and appointed by him an assistant inspector-general in the provost marshal's department; afterward was commandant of general headquarters during the Peninsula and Maryland campaigns. He was an active and vigilant officer, and as such enjoyed the confidence of his superior officers, and no one ever doubted his loyal devotion to his country until the 25th of July, 1863, when, by Special Order No. 331, without notice that nay accusation had been made, and without any form of trial, he was dismissed the service by order of the Secretary of War. Up to that date of his dismissal he has served his country actively and faithfully, most of the time upon the frontier, for twenty-three years, eight months, and eight days.

He was dismissed on a deposition made by Commander Clark H. Wells, charging him with the utterance of disloyal sentiments. The alleged disloyal sentiments were represented by Wells as having been uttered in his presence and in the presence of Maj. Charles J. Whiting, Second United States Cavalry. Major, Whiting, when called upon, denied under oath that Haller made use of the language attributed to him by Wells. Major Haller also denies that he gave utterance to the sentiments to which Wells deposed.

General James Tilton, civil engineer, chief inspector of the water supply of Washington City and Georgetown, D.C., in an affidavit made by him, among other things said:

In 1866 or 1867, being in the city of Washington, I met at the Ebbitt House the officer who was one of the witnesses to the alleged disloyal utterances. I had a conversation with this officer, Commander Clark Wells, U.S.N.

I entered into a full conversation with him upon the subject of Major Haller, and Captain Wells then admitted to me that it was possible that he might have dreamed it, meaning the alleged disloyal utterances or toast said to have been drunk by Major Haller and Whiting of the Army in presence of Captain Wells.

I then apprised Captain Wells that if ever Major Haller succeeded in obtaining a court of inquiry or court-martial upon the charges or allegations under which he had been dismissed I would

---

[59] The city of Washington, D.C.
[60] Gen. Porter commanded the provost marshal's department of the Army of the Potomac from Oct. 1861-Aug. 1862.

certainly, if living, repeat this admission under oath, to which Captain Wells made no dissent, but expressed himself as personally friendly to Major Haller.

Major Haller received from his comrades-in-arms a number of letters bearing testimony to his skill and bravery as an officer and his patriotism during the late war.

Two of theses letters are especially important. One addressed to Major Haller, on February 9, 1874, by Maj. Francis H. Bates (captain and brevet-major, U.S.A., and late first-lieutenant of Major Haller's company), furnishes such unmistakable evidence of Major Haller's devotion to his country at the outbreak of the rebellion that part of it is here given. Among other things, Major Bates says:

I always thought and still think that a great mistake was made somewhere in your case. Knowing as I did the patriotic sentiments which governed all you conversation and actions during the dark days of 1860 and 1861, when we were on the frontiers of civilization at Fort Mojave, New Mexico, and subsequently at San Diego, Cal.; when, as we journeyed toward the settlements and were met and surrounded by the disloyal; when Albert S. Johnson[61] and officers of all grades eagerly threw off their allegiance to our glorious "stars and stripes," and glittering prizes were offered to all who should join in that "Texas band;" when no opposition was offered to their departure, and you and your small command, together with the small dragoon force and quartermaster department at Los Angeles, were nearly all that were left in that section to uphold the honor of our country; remembering all this, I say that if any sentiments of disloyalty had ever animated your breast, it seems to me that this would have been the time for them to have become apparent and betrayed themselves; but you were firm, and our small company, seeing and feeling the determination of their two remaining officers, smothered the rising mutterings that were ever appearing in their midst, stood true and loyal men, and by their firmness, together with the small force at Los Angeles and Yuma, saved, I verily believe, Lower California from joining the ranks of the secession States. There were many deeds of silent heroism and loyalty enacted in those early days upon our frontier, and of which history has taken no notices, which, had they

---

[61] Most likely Maj. Bates refers to Albert S. Johnston who was on the West Coast at the time of the Civil War, resigned his commission and then joined the Confederate Army.

been known, would have gone far toward the protection of the actors in them when accusations were afterward brought against them by superloyalists, whose chief stock in trade consisted in aspersing the character and actions of the true men and patriots of such a true and loyal man as I believe you to have been.

With great respect, I am your friend and former first lieutenant.
F.H. Bates
Captain and Brevet Major, U.S.A

To Granville O. Haller,
Late Major, U.S.A, Ebbitt House, Washington, D.C.

The other letter to which reference was made was written by Gen. John S. Crocker, U.S.A. It affords strong evidence of Major Haller's love of country at the time of the alleged utterance of disloyal sentiments. The letter is all so pertinent to this inquiry that it is given entire below:

Washington, D.C, February 9, 1876

Dear Major: Since our conversation yesterday I have thought of the circumstances connected with your discharge from the Army, and well remember the universal expressions of regret of the officers and men with whom you served at what they deemed the great injustice that was done you. I know the valuable services you rendered your country in her greatest peril and throughout your long career of meritorious service. I distinctly remember your gentlemanly bearing, integrity of character, your bravery and skill as an officer, and therefore I earnestly sympathize with you, and believe the treatment you received was simply cruel. During the war you and myself served a long time at the headquarters of the Army of the Potomac; yourself as commandant of the post at general headquarters and I as colonel commanding the Ninety-third New York Volunteers, the headquarters guard. Thus our official and personal relations were of the most intimate character, and our duties such as brought us together more or less every day and night. Perhaps no officer was more intimately associated with you than myself in the performance of duty. I knew your sentiments, heard your expressions, and was an eye-witness from day to day to your zeal in the cause and to the faithful and efficient manner in which you discharged your onerous duties. Therefore I shall ever be able to bear witness to your bravery and skill as an officer, your untiring industry, your love of country and the good old flag, and your earnest loyalty and real merit.

Hoping and trusting our country will correct the wrongs unwittingly done you, I remain, very respectfully and truly, yours,

John S. Crocker
Brevet Brigadier-General, U.S.A

Maj. Granville O. Haller

Enough has been produced to show that a serious mistake was made somewhere. Here an officer who had served his country for more than twenty-three years, and always with honor and distinction, was summarily dismissed the service, upon the sworn ex-parte statement of a single person, without notice to him, or the opportunity to meet the charges and make a defense. Repeatedly has Major Haller demanded the opportunity to disprove these charges and vindicate his patriotism. Baffled upon every occasion, he has persisted in his demand until the present time. On March 3, 1865, an act of Congress was passed giving officers dismissed by the President a right to a trial by court-martial. The provisions are as follows:

When any officer, dismissed by order of the President, makes in writing an application for trial, setting forth, under oath, that he has been wrongfully dismissed, the President shall, as soon as the necessities of the service may permit, convene a court-martial to try such officer on the charges on which he shall have been dismissed. And if a court-martial is not so convened within six months from the presentation of such application for trial, or if such court, being convened, does not award dismissal or death as the punishment of such officer, the order of dismissal by the President shall be void. (R.S., sec. 1230.)

In the original act, the word "hereafter" occurs before the word "dismissed" in the first line. Whether by the omission of the word "hereafter" it was intended to make the section applicable to cases of dismissal anterior to the passage of the act, it is for the purpose of this case unnecessary to discuss. It has been construed, it would seem not to apply in this case. It, however, does afford a good reason why the relief asked for by Major Haller should be given. There was more reason for such a law when, in the din and excitement of the war, injustice was more apt to be done.

Major Haller demands a right which the Constitution and laws of his country are supposed to secure to every citizen, however high or however humble, a right to a fair and impartial trial by his peers. He has been asking for the privilege of vindicating his loyalty before such a tribunal ever since the order for his dismissal. Your committee believe it to be but justice to him, his friends and family, that he should have such right. If injustice has been done him, he ought to have the privilege of showing it.

The committee report back the joint resolution as amended, with the recommendation that it do pass.

This report states the facts correctly, as shown by the record. Inasmuch as Major Haller has not been afforded the opportunity to meet and disprove the charges, as he has repeatedly requested and urged, and that the act of March 3, 1865, which permits officers dismissed by order of the President to apply for and receive the judgment of a court-martial thereupon has been construed by the War Department not to apply to his case, your committee concur in the report of the House committee, and recommend concurrence of the Senate in the joint resolution.

PROCEEDINGS OF THE COURT OF INQUIRY

FIRST DAY

Proceedings of a Court of Inquire convened at Washington D.C. by the following order:

Headquarters of the Army
Adjutant Generals Office
Washington April 3, 1879

Special Orders No 80
Extract

  5. By direction of the Secretary of War, a Court of Inquiry is hereby appointed in conformity with the requirements of a Joint Resolution of Congress approved March 3rd, 1879, to inquire into and report upon "The matter of the dismissal of Major Granville O Haller, late of the Seventh Infantry, United States Army."
  The Court will assemble May 5, 1879, and the President designates Washington, District of Columbia, as the place of meeting. The Court will report its opinion and finding in accordance with the provisions of the Joint Resolution above cited.
  Detail for the Court
Lieut. Col. H F Clarke Asst Commissary General of Subsistence
Major John Hamilton, 1st Artillery
Major George G Hunt, 1st Cavalry
2nd Lieut G.A. Postley, 3rd Artillery is appointed Recorder of the Court

By Command of Genl. Sherman
E D Townsend
Adjutant General

Washington D C
May 5th, 1879
11,00 o'clock

The Court met pursuant to the above order

Present

Lieut Col. H F Clarke Assistant Commissary General of Subsistence
Major John Hamilton, 1st Artillery
Major George G Hunt, 1st Artillery
2nd Lieut G A Postley, 3rd Arty Recorder

The Court then proceeded to the consideration of the case of Major G O Haller, late of the Seventh Infantry, U S Army, who came before the Court and, having heard the above order read, was asked if he objected to any member therein mentioned. To which he replied in the negative.

The members of the Court were then severally duly sworn by the Recorder, and the Recorder was duly sworn by the President of the Court; all of which oaths were administered in the presence of the accused.

Major Haller then asked permission to introduce as counsel General Charles Ewing, which application the Court granted.

Major Haller then asked, through his counsel, that "all matter which has drifted into the case, since his dismissal, be not considered by the Court," and, to sustain his motion offered the following

"I desire to call the attention of the Court to the fact that this Act of Congress, under which the Court is organized, authorizes it simply to enquire in to the 'matter of the dismissal of Major Granville O Haller late of the 7th Infantry, U S Army,' and to suggest, therefore, that the Court is not authorized to enquire as to the truth of any acts of disloyalty that it may be charged that Major Haller was guilty of subject to the order of his dismissal.

"I make the suggestion simply for the purpose of clearing the record, in this case, of a lot of matter that has, I understand, been placed in the hands of the Judge Advocate, from the files of the War Department, and which I think has nothing to do with the case.

"I also wish it distinctly understood that I do not make this suggestion through fear of the development of any act, on the part of Major Haller, that would brand him as disloyal, for I am abundantly able to prove that he has, during the whole of his life, done nothing that should raise even a suspicion of his loyalty to the government."

The Recorder replied. "These papers are the original papers in the case, and a report of the Judge Advocate, General Dunn dated Aug. 18th 1871. These papers have been submitted to the executive authority as a pail of the "matter of the dismissal of Major Haller." They have been acted upon by this authority and are now referred, by the War Department, to the Court as the record of the case into which they are to enquire. I think that the Court should accept them, or at least permit them to be read, rejecting, after such reading, what it may consider as irrelevant.

Major Haller, through his counsel stated that he would like to examine, as soon as possible, Hon. Levi P. Maish, a witness as to general character. This, though not the ordinary course of procedure, he would like to have adopted as this witness was about leaving town.

The Court then cleared, and, after mature deliberation, opened, and its decision announced by the Recorder that "The Court is of opinion that under the Act of Congress, in pursuance of which it is convened, it has no authority to consider the conduct of Major Haller after his dismissal, except in so far as it may be in rebuttal of the defense against the original charges. In regard to the witness, Hon Levi P. Maish, the Court is of the opinion that it cannot depart from the ordinary mode of procedure in the reference to this witness.

The Counsel for Major Haller then asked that, in as much as Major Haller was not here under charges, that he be permitted to see the papers upon which his dismissal was based.

The Court directed , that Major Haller, not having copies of the papers containing the charges against him, that the Recorder should give him the opportunity to make such examination of them as to enable him to make a proper defense.

The Court then, at 12 o'clock noon, adjourned to meet tomorrow at 11:15 o'clock AM.

SECOND DAY

Washington D.C.
No. 1700 Pennsylvania Avenue
May 6th 1879

The Court met pursuant to adjournment at 11:15 A.M.
Present:
Lieutenant Colonel H. F. Clarke, Assistant Commissary General of Subsistence
Major John Hamilton, 1st Artillery
Major George G. Hunt, 1st Cavalry

2nd Lieutenant G.A. Postley, 3rd Artillery, Recorder

The petitioner and his counsel were also present. The proceedings of the 5th, instant were then read and approved.
The recorder then offered in evidence-
1st: Letter of Captain C.H. Wells, dated Navy Yard Philadelphia, February 17th 1863 to Major Haller U.S.A. Appended herewith (marked "A"). The letter was read and accepted.
2nd: Extract of a letter from Major G. O. Haller, dated January 10th 1863 and a copy of letter, dated York, Penn. February 18th 1863. Appended herewith (marked "B"). The counsel for the petitioner called the attention of the court to the character of the paper about to be read as being an unauthenticated copy.

The Recorder replied that "the paper was sent by Captain Wells to the Secretary of War with the two letters already read, and one about to be read dated March 3rd 1863 reporting Major Haller for disloyal utterances, and through that channel has reached the court for its consideration."

The court was cleared and after mature deliberation opened and the decision announced, by the Recorder, "that the court has decided to receive the paper." The paper was then read and accepted.
3rd: Letter from Captain C.H. Wells, U.S. Navy, dated Navy Yard, Philadelphia, February 20th, 1863; appended herewith, marked "C." Letter read and accepted.
4th: Letter of Captain C.H. Wells, U.S. Navy to Secretary Stanton, dated Navy Yard, Philadelphia, March 3rd 1863. Appended herewith, marked "D." Letter read and accepted.
5th: Letter of C.H. Wells, U.S. Navy to Hon. John Covode[62], dated Navy Yard, Philadelphia, May 1 1863, with endorsement transmitting same to War Department. Appended herewith, marked "E." Letter read and accepted.
6th: Authenticated copy of letter to Hon. Gideon Wells, Secretary of the Navy, from Hon E.M. Stanton, Secretary of War, dated War Department, Washington City, June 6th 1863. Authenticated copy of letter Hon. Gideon Wells, Secretary of the Navy, to Captain C.H. Wells, U.S. Navy, and an authenticated copy of letter from Captain C.H. Wells, U.S. Navy to the Judge Advocate General of the Army, dated U.S. Navy Yard, Philadelphia, June 10,

---

[62] Rep. John Covode, Pennsylvania, 1855-63, 1867-71; died in office 1871. Interment at Methodist Episcopal Cemetery, West Fairfield, PA.

1863. Appended herewith, marked "F." The above letters were read and accepted.

7th: Deposition of Captain C.H. Wells, U.S. Navy, taken before the Judge Advocate General of the Army, and sworn to on the 9th day of July 1863. Appended herewith, marked "G." Deposition read and accepted.

8th: Report of Judge Advocate General Holt, dated Judge Advocate General's Office, Washington 9th July 1863 with endorsement of General Halleck General in Chief. Appended herewith, marked "H." Report read and accepted.

9th: Wrapper about above papers, bearing an endorsement, dated War Department, July 22nd 1863 directing the dismissal of Major G.O. Haller. Appended herewith, marked "K." Read and accepted.

10th: Official copy of Special Order directing the dismissal of Major G.O. Haller. Appended herewith, marked "J." The order was read and accepted.

11th: Memorandum of Solicitor of War Department. Appended herewith, marked "M." Read and accepted.

The Recorder then offered in evidence an official copy of General Orders No 30, dated Head Quarters of the Army, Adjutant General's Office, Washington March 21 1879. Appended herewith marked "O."

The court then asked the counsel for the petitioner for a list of the witnesses he intended to summons, with a statement of what he intended to prove by each. The list was submitted by the counsel of the court. The court was then cleared and after mature deliberation opened and the decision announced by the Recorder "that the list was approved by the court."

The court then at 2.10 O'clock P.M. adjourned to meet tomorrow at 11.15, O'clock, A.M.

THIRD DAY

Washington D.C.
No. 1700 Pennsylvania Avenue
May 7th 1879

The court met pursuant to adjournment at 11.15 O'clock A.M this day

Present
Lieutenant Colonel H. F. Clarke, Assistant Commissary General of Subsistence
Major John Hamilton, 1st Artillery
Major George G. Hunt, 1st Cavalry
2nd Lieutenant G.A. Postley, 3rd Artillery, Recorder

 The Petitioner and his counsel were also present. The proceedings of the 6th instant were then read and approved.
 Michael D. Murphy, a clerk, authorized to act as such for this court by the Secretary of War, was then duly sworn by the Recorder according to law.
 The Recorder here announced that the case for the Government here rest.
 The counsel for the petitioner then submitted a letter from Major General A.E. Burnside, dated March 28th 1863 whose signature was recognized by the court. Letter appended herewith marked "P." The letter was read by the recorder and accepted.
 Major F.H. Bates, U.S. Army, retired, a witness for the petitioner was then duly sworn by the Recorder and testified as follows:
 Question by the Recorder: What is your name and position in the service?
 Answer: F.H. Bates, Captain and Brevet-Major U.S. Army retired.
 Question by the Recorder: Do you recognize the petitioner before the court?
 Answer: Yes, Major Granville O. Haller, late of the Army.
 Question by the petitioner: Were you an officer in the United States Army in the 1860 and 1861?
 Answer: Yes, in 1860 and 1861
 Question: State briefly your services with Major Haller in 1860 and 1861.
 Answer: I was 1st Lieutenant in Captain and Brevet-Major G.O. Haller's Company "I", 4th U.S. Infantry, from the letter part of November 1854 to the 14th of May 1861 and acting in the same capacity and present with the company until it joined the regiment at Washington, in December 1861, with the exception of a few months.
 I was on duty with the company and on intimate relations with Major Haller from December 1860 to December 1861. At the outbreak of the rebellion at Fort Mojave, New Mexico, and

subsequently till we embarked for New York, about the 1st of December 1861 at San Diego, California. We reached San Diego about June 1861.

Nearly all, if not all, of the army officers serving on the Pacific Coast so far as I know, who were appointed from Southern States, and some whose birth and education were in the North, conspicuously among the latter, Lieutenant Ives, of the Topographical Engineers, and Lieutenant Riley, of the 6th Infantry, handed in their resignation and started for the Southern Confederacy.

During the Summer of 1861, the state of affairs was freely discussed at all times, and officers then and there took their stand for and against the Union and made a final decision as to there future course.

I remember no words and know of no acts of Major Haller during all this exciting period which could in any way be considered opposed to the words and acts of an officer, thoroughly and decidedly patriotic and loyal to the Government and Union of the United States.

For sometime one company comprised the only troops stationed between Los Angeles and Fort Yuma.

The prevailing sentiment of the people of San Diego and vicinity was a disunion sentiment; we know not how many of our own men were disaffected. Haller used every expedient to ascertain the individual opinion and sentiment of the now commissioned officers and men; and by inforcing such discipline used every precaution to guard against any attempt that might be made to revolt against his authority.

Rumors were constantly coming in that parties were organizing for the purpose of overcoming our weak garrison appropriating our supplies and occupying our position; Haller was always alert to adopt any means for the purpose of thwarting the effects that such rumors might have on the minds of the enlisted men of the command.

CROSS EXAMINATION

Question by the Recorder: What you have stated occurred in 1860, did it not?
Answer: Between the Spring of 1861 and December 1861

Question: Did you again serve with Major Haller during the interval between the occurrence of these events and the period of his dismissal?

Answer: I served in the Army of the Potomac until after July 1862 and saw Major Haller frequently.

Question: Did you serve with him intimately during that period?

Answer: No.

Question: Were you so associated with him during that period that you could decidedly pronounce upon his disposition as to loyalty or disloyalty at that time?

Answer: I can say that I neither saw or heard anything against him that would change my previous statement.

Question: From the nature of your association at that time could not many things have happened bearing upon his loyalty which you would not have known?

Answer: I think I would have know anything that would have occurred. Having been so long associated with him I was anxious to know all about him.

Question: To give some idea of the intimacy of your association with him will you please state as nearly as you can about at what intervals you were in the habit of seeing him?

Answer: Major General McClellan's headquarters was usually pitched in the vicinity of the regular troops with which I served and I would frequently see Haller to pass the compliments of the day but not to have any extended conversation with him sometimes once a week and sometimes once in two weeks or more.

Question: Are you then quite sure that Major Haller could not have entertained disloyal sentiments during that time without your knowing of it?

Answer: Yes, as certain as it is possible for a man to be.

Question: During the time that you were meeting the petitioner in the neighborhood of Headquarters, Army of the Potomac what impression did he make upon you as to zeal, in the discharge of his proper duties; was his post sincere?

Answer: I considered him one of the most zealous and hard working officers in the Army of the Potomac.

Question: Did you hear any rumors of the disloyalty of Major Haller prior to January 1st 1863?

Answer: To the best of my recollection I never heard a word until after he was dismissed.

Colonel John S. Crocker, a witness for petitioner, being duly sworn by the Recorder, testified as follows:

Question by the Recorder: What is your name and what position have you held in the service. What is your present occupation?

Answer: My name is John S. Crocker. I was Colonel of the 93rd Regiment N.Y. Vols and Brevet-Brigadier General of Volunteers. My present occupation is Ward of the United States Jail which have held for the past two years.

Question: Do you recognize the petitioner before the court?

Answer: Yes, Major Granville O. Haller U.S. Army.

Question by the Petitioner: How long did you serve in the Army of the Potomac, during the War of the Rebellion, and what duty were you on with your regiment in the latter part of 1862?

Answer: I joined the Army of the Potomac, with my regiment about the last of January 1862, and continued to serve with that Army until September 1864.

I was on duty at the General Headquarters, Army of the Potomac during the latter part of 1862, and for a year or town as Commandant of the Headquarters Guard, and during that time had an officer detailed from my regiment as Major Haller's Post Adjutant. Major Haller being Commandant of the Post General Headquarters.

Question: How long and how intimately were you acquainted with Major Haller at Headquarters Army of the Potomac?

Answer: I first formed the acquaintance of Major Haller at Headquarters Army of the Potomac in August 1862 and was intimately associated with him in the discharge of his duty from that time until he was relieved in March 1863.

During all that time I saw him every day and was often with him during the greater part of the and late at night.

Question: Do you know why he was relieved from duty at Headquarters?

Answer: About January or February 1863, he had something on his face, we thought it was a cancer and that he needed medical treatment. He went to Washington for that treatment; I saw him upon his return and his face seemed to be better; after a time it grew worse and he was finally relieved from duty at Headquarters upon that account.

Question: What was his reputation as to loyalty during that period?

Answer: I believed him to be thoroughly loyal and patriotic. I always found him earnest and efficient in the discharge of his duties. I never hear his loyalty questioned until after his dismissal.

Question: Did you ever hear anyone but Lieutenant Wells question Major Haller's loyalty?

Answer: I never did.

CROSS EXAMINATION

Question by the Recorder: About how long was Major Haller absent from Headquarters during the winter of 1862 or 1863, prior to the time of his being relieved?

Answer: About a week or two. I was not absent myself more than a day or two.

The counsel for the petitioner asked that the court be adjourned until May 10th 1879 as he had no further witnesses and did not think that he could have them here before Saturday May 10 1879.

The court then at 2.30 O'clock P.M. adjourned to meet again at 10 O'clock A.M. on Saturday May 10 1879.

FOURTH DAY

Washington D.C.
No. 1700 Pennsylvania Avenue
May 10th 1879

The court meet pursuant to adjournment at 10 O'clock A.M this day

Present
Lieutenant Colonel H. F. Clarke, Assistant Commissary General of Subsistence
Major John Hamilton, 1st Artillery
Major George G. Hunt, 1st Cavalry
2nd Lieutenant G.A. Postley, 3rd Artillery, Recorder

The Petitioner and his counsel were also present. The proceedings of the 7th instant were then read and approved.

Major General D.N. Couch, a witness for the petitioner, being duly sworn according to law, testified as follows:

Question by the Recorder: What is your name, rank and present occupation?
Answer: Darius N. Couch, I was Major General United States Volunteers; my present residence, Norwalk Connecticut.
Question: Do you recognize the petitioner before the court, if so, please state whom he is?
Answer: Yes, Major Granville O. Haller whom I know very well.
Question by the Petitioner: When did you enter the military service of the United States, and what commissions have you held?
Answer: I graduated at West Point in 1846 and left the service in 1855. Was Colonel of Massachusetts Volunteers June 1861; Brigadier General of Volunteers 1861 and Major General of Volunteers from June 1862 to June 1865.
Question: Where were serving in June and July 1863?
Answer: I commanded the Department of the Susquehanna, Pennsylvania, headquarters at Harrisburgh[63].
Question: Did any officer of the Regular Army voluntarily place himself under your orders at Harrisburgh, Pa, at the this time and if so, please name him?
Answer: I think that there were several officers who did. A very large number of regular and volunteer. I can not say positively if Major Haller volunteered or not; I presumed he did.
Question: What duty did you order him to perform?
Answer: He had orders to see that my order in reference to moving stock was complied with in my district; also to organize and send out scouts in the direction of the enemy; to encourage the people to volunteer and obey the Governor's orders on that subject; to send me all the information that would be necessary for me to know, and in case of emergency to do anything that the Major General Commanding the Department would deem it necessary for him to do.

I present two orders (appended herewith marked "Q" & "R"). These orders I recognize as original orders. The orders were read and accepted.

I also present a letter dated Headquarters York District; York, Pennsylvania June 19th 1863 this report being from Major Haller to

---

[63] This is how Harrisburg, PA is spelled in the transcripts

me in reference to operations at that time. Letter appended herewith marked "S". The letter was read and accepted.

Question: Did Major Haller discharge this duty to your satisfaction and how did you regard him?

Answer: Major Haller's service while on duty with me was wholly and entirely satisfactory. I do not think that there were any of the fighting Generals of the Army of the Potomac if they had been in York, in the position of Major Haller that could have done any better than he did. I thought so at that time and I think so now.

Question: Did you ever hear it said that Major Haller was disloyal prior to the time you heard of his dismissal?

Answer: Not to my remembrance. When I heard that Major Haller was accused of disloyalty I was as much surprised and astounded as though I had been accused of the same crime or any other person in the United States.

Question: Were you in such communication with the people of York, outside of Major Haller, so that you could have heard of his disloyalty had it been known or suspected by the people of York?

Answer: York was a strategic point. It covered the approaches to Columbia Bridge, on of the important crossings of the Susquehanna and it gave me more anxiety possibility than any other point in Pennsylvania excepting Chambersburg.

At this time I was in hourly communication with York, receiving much information through Governor Curtin and other state officials and as Major Haller was my representative, at York, had there been any doubts as to his loyalty by the people thereof I should have heard of it as once. I had the fullest confidence in Major Haller while he was on duty there. At this time no person in the United States could have judged of Major Haller so well as myself.

General Couch here submitted, an order dated Headquarters Department of the Susquehanna, July 15th 1863, appended herewith marked "T". The order was read and accepted.

CROSS EXAMINATION

Question by the Recorder: Do you know anything of Major Haller beyond the knowledge given by your experience with him at Harrisburgh and vicinity?

Answer: On the Peninsula. I simply knew him as aide-de-camp attached to the staff of General McClellan.

Question: Do you consider that your intercourse with Major Haller was that familiar nature during that time that you could have discovered sentiments of disloyalty had they existed with him?

Answer: I do not know how I can answer that question except by saying that I can not conceive that a man could do what Major Haller did for the country and at the same time be disloyal.

Question by the court: What means had you of knowing of his presence in Harrisburgh (and hence ordering him) other than that of his voluntary report to you?

Answer: I have no doubt that he came up from York voluntarily. I may have sent for him. I had no roster within my reach which would have informed me of his presence at York. I know no one in Pennsylvania at that time and had to take the advice of Governor Curtin and others as to men; they may have informed me of Major Haller's presence at York.

Levi Maish, a witness for the petitioner, being duly sworn, according to the law, testified as follows:

Question by the Recorder: What is your name, occupation and residence?

Answer: Levi Maish, lawyer by profession. I was colonel of the 130th Pennsylvania Volunteers during the late war. I live in York, Pennsylvania, lived there during the war and live their now.

Question: Do you recognize the petitioner before the court?

Answer: Yes, I recognize the petitioner as Major Haller.

Question by the petitioner: How long have you known Major Haller?

Answer: I have known Major Haller personally since June 1863. I have known of him perhaps five years before that.

Question: What was Major Haller's reputation in York for loyalty during the war and what is it now?

Answer: I would say in answer to that question that before Captain Wells made the charge that you are trying him on I have never heard his loyalty questioned in York or elsewhere.

Since this charge has been made the predominate sentiment is that Major Haller is a loyal citizen, a patriotic man and I have never met a man who believed the charges made against him to be true.

Question: Had Major Haller been know in York prior to the Wells charge as a disloyal man; would you have known it?

Answer: Yes, I believe I would have heard of it, if he had been a disloyal man. I would add that if a regular army officer had expressed disloyal sentiments it would have been apt to have been generally discussed during that time.

Question: Were you in York, Pennsylvania when the Confederate soldiers invaded Pennsylvania in 1863. Did you see Haller there. Did you know what he did upon hearing that the enemy were in Pennsylvania?

Answer: I was in York, Pennsylvania, in the summer of 1863 when Lee invaded Pennsylvania. I knew and frequently met Major Haller during that time. Major Haller and I visited General Couch at Harrisburgh together for the purpose of receiving instructions from him in reference to military movements.

In pursuance of such instructions, I know Major Haller to have been at that time active and zealous in communicating information to headquarters; arousing the people to the danger of the invasion, advising them to save their cattle, stock & etc. In many of these things I cooperated with him.

Question: Were you and Major Haller ordered to report to General Couch or did you do it voluntarily?

Answer: I did not know whether Major Haller was ordered to report or whether he reported voluntarily.

I received a telegram from a prominent citizen of York, at Baltimore, when I was on my way home from Virginia, where I had been to see a brother who served under Milroy[64] and was reported to be wounded, informing me that Governor Curtin requested my presence at Harrisburgh to assist in defending the State against invasion. I went directly from Baltimore to Harrisburgh where I met Major Haller and he and I called upon General Couch as already stated. Major Haller and I were directed by General Couch to raise some emergency men which I was doing until the appearance of the rebels at York put a stop to that manner of recruiting.

CROSS EXAMINATION

Question by the Recorder: After the commencement of war what were your opportunities of judging of Major Haller's loyalty or disloyalty?

---

[64] Gen. Robert Milroy, at that time commanding 2nd Division, 8th Army Corps

Answer: Major Haller was a resident of York, I believe, for a time during the war prior to his dismissal. It was his home he had a good many relations being there whom I know very well and I was acquainted generally with his acquaintances. I will say, therefore, that if Major Haller, a regular army officer, had been disloyal or expressed sentiments against the Union cause I would have been very likely to have heard it. This is the foundation for my opinion.

Question: You did not live or associate with him during the period of from the commencement of the war until the time of his dismissal except so far as you have stated?

Answer: I did not.

Question: You state that you would have known if Major Haller's disloyalty had such disloyalty existed. Please state how you would have known it.

Answer: In answer to that question I will say that I would have been likely to hear of Major Haller's disloyalty in York where he lived for a time, where he was well know, where he had numerous acquaintances, had he been a disloyal man. I do not wish to be understood as having said unequivocally, as the question implies, that I would have known of Major Haller's disloyalty had it existed. I say under the circumstances already stated by me that I would have been as likely to hear of it as other persons occupying the same relation to him.

I would further say that I know nothing whatever of my personal knowledge of Major Haller's loyalty or disloyalty excepting what I have already said about his services during the invasion.

Question: You admit then that Major Haller might have been disloyal without your knowing it?

The counsel for the petitioner said "I object to this question. The witness has made no such admission and if he had it would be of no value before this court. He has stated the relations existing between himself and Major Haller and has said that so far as his knowledge goes Major Haller was a loyal man

"Here his ability to gain evidence as to loyalty or disloyalty ends. He is no more competent to say whether Haller could have been disloyal without his knowing it than this court is. The witness admission that Major Haller could or could not have been disloyal without his knowing it would only be his opinion of what could or could not be in state of facts that are before the court and it is the exclusive prerogative of them to judge if on this state of facts Major

Haller might have been disloyal as charged. The witness is not an expert as to disloyalty; his opinion on that subject is not evidence."

The Recorder replied as follows: The witness has testified as to his knowledge of Major Haller's loyalty or disloyalty more positively I think than the counsel's statement indicates and he has given his means and opportunities for obtaining this knowledge. These do not seem to me of that character on which could be properly based a positive opinion, and I wish, by an admission from the witness that his sources of information are unreliable, to show that such is a fact.

The court was then cleared and after mature deliberation opened and the decision of the count announced by the Recorder "that the court sustains the objection of the counsel."

Question: Did Captain Wells ever express to you any opinion of Major Haller's loyalty. Did you ask him his opinion about it?
Answer: I have no recollection that Captain Wells ever expressed an opinion to me about Major Haller's loyalty, nor do I recollect of ever having asked him anything about it.

Mr. Peter Bentz a witness for the petitioner was then duly sworn according to law by the Recorder and testified as follows:
Question by the Recorder: What is your name, occupation and residence?
Answer: My name is Peter Bentz, a Professor of Music residing in York, Pennsylvania.
Question: Do you recognize the petitioner before the court?
Answer: Yes, I have always known him as Granville O. Haller.
Question by the petitioner: How long have you lived in York, Penn.?
Answer. Ever since I was born in 1830.
Question: How long have you known Major Haller?
Answer: My first recollection of Granville O. Haller was during the time of the Mexican War.
Question: Have you ever known Major Haller guilty of any disloyal acts or expressions?
Answer: Never.

Question: Was Major Haller "noted for his disloyalty in York, Pennsylvania" in 1862 or 1863 or since?
Answer: He was not so noted.
Question: With what political party did you act in 1862 and 1863 and have you acted with it since?
Answer: I have been a Republican since the existence of that party and am now.

CROSS EXAMINATION

Question by the Recorder: Was Major Haller's loyalty questioned in York Pennsylvania prior to his dismissal?
Answer: I have never known Major Haller's loyalty questioned by anyone in York, excepting Clark H. Wells now Captain United States Navy.
Question: Was Major Haller's position among the citizens of York, Pennsylvania, such that his conduct and expressions of loyalty or disloyalty would have been likely to have been generally discussed?
Answer: Yes, I never heard any man woman or child in York question Haller's loyalty previous to the charges made by Clark H. Wells.
Question: Was Major Haller's conduct during that period ever generally discussed in any form?
Answer: It was spoken of the same as that of any officer of the army holding the same position that he did, would be.
Question: Was Major Haller prominently known in York during the war?
Answer: I think he was.

The court then at 2 O'clock adjourned to meet again on Monday May the 12th at 11.15 O'clock A.M.

FIFTH DAY

Washington D.C.
No. 1700 Pennsylvania Avenue
May 12th 1879

The court meet pursuant to adjournment at 11.15 O'clock A.M this day

Present
Lieutenant Colonel H. F. Clarke, Assistant Commissary General of Subsistence
Major John Hamilton, 1st Artillery
Major George G. Hunt, 1st Cavalry
2nd Lieutenant G.A. Postley, 3rd Artillery, Recorder

The Petitioner and his counsel were also present. The proceedings of the 10th instant were then read and approved.

   The petitioner Major Granville O. Haller a witness in his own behalf was then duly sworn according to the law and testified as follows:

   Question by the counsel: Please state to the court when you entered the military service of the United States and generally when you served up to the date of the order of your dismissal.
   Answer: I was commissioned 2nd Lieutenant 4th Infantry November 17th 1839; in 1840 I joined my regiment at Fort Gibson; in 1841 entered Florida; 1842 went to Jefferson Barracks, brigaded with the 3rd Infantry; 1844 became part of the Army of Observation on the borders of Texas under General Taylor; in 1845 entered Texas, served through all the battles until we occupied Monterrey. In battles I was on the staff of Lieutenant Colonel Garland but had charge of the entire Commissary Stores for the army.
   When ordered to Vera Cruz I surrendered the staff duties and took command of Co. "I" 4th Infantry and served with that company through all the actions until we occupied the City of Mexico. Served on the Lakes a short time; in 1852 proceeded to the Pacific Coast was engaged in several campaigns against the Indians in the State of Oregon and in Washington Territory and had several engagements with the Indians. Served in the San Juan embroglio and was at Fort

Mojave, Utah Territory at the breaking of the Secession Movement; thence I was stationed at San Diego California from thence ordered to Washington City with the 4th Infantry.

Upon my arrival in Washington I found that I had been promoted to Major in the 4th Infantry; That regiment being prisoners of war and stationed on the Lakes I sought active duty; was appointed Assistant Provost Marshall General under General Andrew Porter of the United State Army.

In a day or two after we commenced our march from Fortress Monroe, Virginia, I was detailed as Commandant at the General Headquarters by General McClellan, commanding the Army of the Potomac. This entailed upon me a double duty of Assistant Provost Marshal General and Commandant of General Headquarters.

I served throughout General McClellan's term, in command of that army, then General Burnside's and General Hooker's until an obstinate attack of Impetigo, on my left cheek induced me, upon the recommendations of the doctors, to seek indoor service.

I was then appointed, by General Fry[65], Provost Marshal General for the State of Maryland, but Governor Bradford of Maryland, having previously recommended some person for the office to the Secretary of War, regarded my appointment as a discourtesy to him. I reported this promptly to General Fry who wished me to suspend my duties until I heard from him. He authorized me to stop in York Pennsylvania until I received orders from him.

I think on that day, or the day after, Lee entered Pennsylvania with his army, whereupon I hastened to Harrisburg, Pennsylvania and reported to General D.N. Couch my circumstances the position I was in at the time (awaiting orders) and would be glad to assist him if I could.

I remember going in company with Colonel Maish early on one occasion to receive orders. I remained in service with General Couch until he announced that the exigencies of the service requiring my assistance was over.

While making my report for mustering volunteers into the service, liabilities for horses in field operations & etc., in the month of July 1863 I was suddenly informed that I was dismissed the service.

---

[65] General James Fry, first Provost Marshall General of the US Army, 1863-66; Adjutant General's Office, 1866-1881

Question: Did you protest against your dismissal and did you request copies of the charges on which you were dismissed and did you get a hearing or were you furnished with the charges by the Department?[66]

Answer: My first effort was to request the Department to allow me to see the nature of the allegations against me; my applications were positively refused. I then presented a paper showing that I was not disloyal and requested that I might be allowed to go before a General Court Martial or Court of Inquiry to investigate the matter; this paper was delivered in person to the Honorable the Secretary of War by the Honorable J.P. Black of York, Pennsylvania who upon his return to York, Pennsylvania informed me that the Secretary told him that he would answer it and to which I never received any answer. After waiting for a reasonable time I addressed the War Department asking that I might be permitted to go before the Military Board of which General Ricketts[67] U.S.A. was the President to have my conduct investigated but I never received an answer to that communication.

I have failed to get a hearing until by the Act of the late Congress this court was authorized to enquire into the matter of my dismissal. See letter appended marked "U."

Question: Did Lieutenant Commander Wells of the U.S. Navy accompany you to Army Headquarters in the field in December 1862 and did he do so by your invitation?

Answer: Lieutenant Commander Wells did accompany me to Headquarters Army of the Potomac, then at Falmouth opposite Fredericksburg in December 1862 but not at my invitation.

Question: How was this visit brought about?

Answer: He expressed a wish to go to the headquarters to pay General Franklin[68], U.S Army a visit and asked if he might go with me.

Question: Did you and Lieutenant Commander Wells make a visit to any part of the lines of the army prior to the night on which Lieut. Cmdr Wells refused to remain in your tent and if so, please state what occurred on your way back to General Headquarters.

---

[66] referring to the War Department
[67] General James Ricketts served in numerous combat commands during the Civil War; sat on the court that forced General Fitz-John Porter out of the army.
[68] General William Franklin

Answer: He and I visited Fredericksburg in the afternoon I think of the day after we arrived in camp the enemy's cannon were firing pretty lively at the time and it was getter well along towards evening. Wishing to be in camp at retreat I proposed to cross over the pontoon bridge, get the horsed and bring them to the bridge and suggested to Lieut Commander Wells that he could remain until the guns got heated, when the enemy would cease firing and then he could cross in safety; he remained there until the firing had ceased, came over and met me at the bridge where I remained until he joined me.

Question: Did you, on the night referred to by Lieut. Commander Wells, in his affidavit, that has been offered and accepted in this case, propose a toast? And if so, please repeat it if you can.

Answer: Having heated the water and made a hot toddy as I handed the glasses to the officer, I gave this toast, 'Here's to the Constitution as it is, the Union as it was.'

Question: What other toast did you propose?

Answer: None other, I gave but one.

Question: Did you not offer the toast, 'Here's to a Southern and Northern Confederation whilst Lincoln is President' or words to that effect?

Answer: I did not.

Question: Are you perfectly certain as to this?

Answer: As certain as that I am sitting here now.

CROSS EXAMINATION

Question by the Recorder: When Captain Wells forwarded to Secretary Stanton a report of the disloyal toast which he says you proposed did he not at that time send you a copy of his letter?

Answer: On the 4th of March 1863 he enclosed a copy of his letter to the Secretary of War of March 3 1863 to me.

Question: Did you take any action in the matter or attempt any defense up to the time of your dismissal?

The question was objected to by the counsel for the petitioner on the ground that 'No charge had been made against Major Haller up to that time therefore no defense could be made.'

The Recorder stated 'That he merely wished to show in what manner Major Haller looked upon the charge made by showing what action he took to refute it.'

The objection was not sustained by the court.

Answer: As soon as I learned that Lieutenant Commander Wells labored under hallucinations I consulted with Major Whiting who was present at the time; he promised me that he would write to Lieut. Comdr Wells and correct his impression upon the subject. At that time Major Whiting was in Washington upon a Court Marital and being busy seemed to have over looked his promise.

When I received this letter of Wells to the Secretary of War of the 3rd of March 1863 I showed it to Major Whiting and he supposed that it would be referred to General Hooker, who then commanded the Army of the Potomac, who would call him in who knew all about it and that he would explain the whole matter.

Question: Did you ever employ James S. Shinck(?) attorney in your behalf in this case?

The counsel for the petitioner said 'I object to the question as it does not relate to the matter of the dismissal of Major Haller and is not in rebuttal of the statement made by him.'

The Recorder answered that 'Testimony had been admitted of a date subsequent to the time of the dismissal. Therefore it was admissible to cross examine upon that time. Major Haller has testified as to a part of the action taken by himself to effect his restoration to rank, therefore, I think that I have the right to show all of the attempts made by him. I think that I have the same right to show all of these acts. Testimony to part having been introduced as I have to call for the production of an entire letter or document when an extract is offered in evidence.'

The court was cleared and after mature deliberation opened and the decision announced by the Recorder 'that the objection was sustained.'

Question: What was the paper referred to in your examination as presented by your showing that you were not disloyal?

Answer: Merely a letter from me to the Honorable the Secretary of War.

Question: Do you consider that you are the author of a pamphlet superscribed *The dismissal of Major Granville O. Haller of the regular army of the United States, by order of the Secretary of War in Special Orders No 331 of July 25th 1863; also a brief memoir of his military services and a few observations*?

Objected to the counsel for the petitioner. The counsel stated 'The fact of having written the pamphlet- that had nothing to do with the question before the court under the Special Act of Congress directing its creation and in addition the pamphlet referred to is of a subsequent date to that of the dismissal all of which matter the court had ruled it will not receive.'

The Recorder then replied, 'I merely asked the question in order to prove the document as I propose asking the court hereafter to admit it in rebuttal. In addition to this, I give the same reason to sustain my question as given for the previous question.'

The court was then cleared and after mature deliberation opened and the decision of the court was announced by the Recorder 'that the objection was sustained.'

Question by the court: What was your condition as to sobriety when the so called toast was given?

Answer: I believe I was sound in mind and body when I gave the toast. Physically and mentally sober.

Question: Name who were present when the said toast was given.

Answer: Lieutenant Commander Clark H. Wells U.S. Navy, Major Charles J Whiting 5th Cavalry and myself.

Major Charles J. Whiting a witness for the petitioner being duly sworn according to law testified as follows:

Question by the Recorder: What is your name and where do you reside?

Answer: Charles J. Whiting, a resident of Castine, Maine

Question: Do you recognize the petitioner before the court and if so please state whom he is?

Answer: Yes as Granville O. Haller, formerly Major, 7th Infantry.

Question by the petitioner: When did you enter the military service of the United States?

Answer: I graduated from West Point in 1835.

Question: Did you serve in the Army of the Potomac during any part of the War of the Rebellion? And if so, for what length of time and in what capacity during the winter of 1862 and 1863?

Answer: I served with the Army of the Potomac from the commencement of the Rebellion until 1863.

Question: Were you personally acquainted with Major Haller? And what duty, if any, was he on in the Army of the Potomac in the winter of 1862 and 1863.

Answer: I was personally acquainted with Major Haller who was in the winter of 1862 and 1862 commanding the Headquarters Guard, Army of the Potomac.

Question: What was Major Haller's reputation as a solider and particularly as to loyalty?

Answer: I never heard aught against him. I may add that he was a very active duty office.

Question: Did you in December 1862 meet any officer of the Navy in Major Haller's tent?

Answer: I did. I met an officer to whom I was introduced by Major Haller as Lieutenant Wells, United States Navy.

Question: Do you remember if during the evening in question you gentlemen exchanged views on any topics of general public interest and if so, please state some of them?

Answer: Yes, we were discussing the removal of General McClellan and the President's Emancipation Proclamation.

Question: Did you take as much part in the discussion of these questions as Major Haller did?

Answer: I think I took considerable more.

Question: Did Lieutenant Comdr Wells declare the sentiments you uttered in the discussion of these topics were disloyal or did he declare because of these sentiments he would not remain with you gentlemen over night?

Answer: No.

Question: After you had discussed the questions you have named was there any conversation relative to any matters personal to either of you gentlemen and if so what?

Answer: Lieutenant Wells hinted to Haller that he might be in some other command besides there at Headquarters and Haller retorted by asking why he had not crossed a certain bridge.

Question: What, if anything, did Wells do or say in answer?

Answer: He commenced packing up his carpet sack or valise and said he would not sleep with Haller and asked if he could go and sleep with me; he went with me.

Question: When did you learn that Mr. Wells was an officer of the Navy?

Answer: When I first entered the tent, I was introduced to him, by Major Haller, as Lieutenant Wells, United States Navy.

Question: Did you on the night in question not anytime there after say to Lieutenant Commander Wells that you did not know he was an officer of the Navy or you would not have talked as you did in Major Haller's tent?

Answer: No sir

Question: Did you propose a toast or did Lieut. Commander Wells propose one that evening?

Answer: Neither of us did.

Question: When drinking the 'Hot Scotch' that Major Haller prepared for you gentlemen did he propose a toast and if so please repeat it if you can.

Answer: 'Here's to the Constitution as it is, and the Union as it was.'

Question: Did you hear Major Haller also propose as a toast 'Here's to a Southern and a Northern Confederation under Lincoln's administration' or anything like it?

Answer: No sir

Question: Are you perfectly certain as to this?

Answer: I am positive that Major Haller never proposed such a toast.

Question: Please state how it comes that you can now, fifteen years after the scene in Major Haller's tent, swear so positively as to what took place that night.

Answer: My mind was particularly called to it, shortly after it occurred, by Major Haller informing me that Wells proposed preferring charges against him and also twice since my attention has been called to it. I never think of Major Haller without thinking of it.

CROSS EXAMINATION

Question by the Recorder: You say that you did not hear but one toast proposed by Major Haller that evening. Were you so situation that you can say positively that he did propose but one toast?

Answer: I can, there were but three of us in the wall tent and I remained there all the time until I took Lieutenant Wells out to my tent.

Question: Major Haller had been entertaining his friends generally in a social manner that evening had he not?

Answer: Yes, there was a party of gentlemen leaving the tent just as I went in.

Question: At what time was it that this controversy between Major Haller and Captain Wells occurred?

Answer: Late at night; between ten and eleven o'clock.

Question: to what extent did you drink that evening?

Answer: I did not take more than one or two drinks. There was more talking than drinking.

Question: Are you quite sure that you had not been drinking to an extent such as to materially affect your understanding or appreciation of the conversation between Haller and Wells?

Answer: No, sir, I fully appreciated it.

Question: Were you dismissed from the service for disloyalty on or about 1863; after the dismissal of Major Haller?

Answer: Yes, I was summarily dismissed by the Secretary of War.

Question: Under what circumstances were you dismissed?

Answer: I was summarily dismissed by order of the Secretary of War on the charge of disloyalty and speaking disrespectfully of the President of the United States. I applied to go before the court that was then in session for the trial of officers summarily dismissed upon their own application and the Secretary of War refused my application for the reason that he did approve the Act of Congress authorizing it.

General George H. Thomas happened to come to Washington at that time; he was my major and knew me well asked me if I wished to be re-instated. I told him 'no', that the War Department threatened to try me and I wanted them to do so. He told me to write such a letter as I wished to the President that he would see that he did receive it. I stepped into Willards Hotel, wrote the letter and General Thomas put his endorsement upon it and the next day I was ordered before the court. The charges which were sent to the court to try me on said nothing about disloyalty. There were only three charges. 'Speaking disrespectfully of the President of the United States,' 'Conduct unbecoming an officer and a gentleman' and 'conduct prejudicial to good order and military discipline.' All based upon the same specifications.

The President of the United States, Mr. Johnson, told me that the court has examined Mr. Lincoln for dismissing me, but had recommended me to him; that he has received the proceedings himself and had made up his mind to restore me to my old rank in the army. Which he did.

The counsel for the petitioner then said: 'If the court please I wish to call Colonel Samuel Ross, United States Army, retired, before introducing him I desire to say that I propose to prove by him that Major General Halleck was Chief of Staff to the President of the United States previous and subsequent to the date of the order announcing Major Haller's dismissal from the Army. That sometime thereafter General Halleck said to Colonel Ross that 'Major Haller was not guilty of the crime for which he was dismissed,' and that he further said that, as Chief of Staff, he by direction of the President attended Cabinet meetings, that immediately after the adjournment of a Cabinet meeting just subsequent to the promulgation of the order announcing Haller's dismissal, President Lincoln said to Mr Secretary of War Stanton 'Look here Stanton I don't think you should have dismissed Major Haller presumptuously in as much as you can court marital an officer for making water against a stump when a lady can see him with a telescope. What is the use of dismissing a man without a trial?' That had he Halleck been Secretary of War he would have regarded what the President said as an order and would at one have revoked the order dismissing Haller.

'The act which you are assembled directs you to inquire into the matter of the dismissal of Major Haller and as to the Recorder introduced and you have accepted evidence tending to prior the dismissal, I believe that I have the right to rebut the evidence and if possible prove that Haller was not dismissed in pursuance of law and therefore not dismissed at all; and I consequently offer this witness as the best evidence it is possible for me to present to you of the fact that the President of the United States did not order, or direct, or even consent to the dismissal of Major Haller.'

The Recorder objected to the introduction of such testimony on the ground that it would be, if admitted, hearsay evidence to disapprove a fact established by documentary evidence.

The court was then cleared and after mature deliberation opened and the decision of the court was announced by the Recorder: "that the testimony would not be admitted."

The Recorder moved that he be directed by the court to take the disposition of General Schenck, on proper notice to the counsel for the petitioner. He stated that General Schenck was sick and unable to attend the court. The court so ordered.

The court then at 3 O'clock P.M. adjourned to meet tomorrow the 13 of May at 11.15 O'clock A.M.

SIXTH DAY

Washington D.C.
No. 1700 Pennsylvania Avenue
May 13 1879

The court meet pursuant to adjournment at 11.15 O'clock A.M this day

Present
Lieutenant Colonel H. F. Clarke, Assistant Commissary General of Subsistence
Major John Hamilton, 1st Artillery
Major George G. Hunt, 1st Cavalry
2nd Lieutenant G.A. Postley, 3rd Artillery, Recorder

The Petitioner and his counsel were also present. The proceedings of the 12 instant were then read and approved.

The Recorder then stated that he had called upon General Schenck the previous evening. That General Schenck had then sufficiently recovered to be able to drive out but not to ascend two flights of stairs.
That General Schenck had agreed to meet General Ewing and the Recorder at the Secretary of War office at 11 O'clock this A.M. That General Ewing and he had gone to the office and had failed to find General Schenck; that they had waited there until the time fixed for the assembling of the court and that up to that time General Schenck had not arrived. The Recorder asked that he be permitted to take the deposition of the General after the adjournment of the court today.
The request was granted by the court.
The Recorder then stated: 'I offer in evidence a pamphlet of 82 pages *The dismissal of Major Granville O. Haller of the regular army of the United States, by order of the Secretary of War in Special*

Orders No 331 of July 25th 1863; also a brief memoir of his military services and a few observations. In offering the document he stated that 'If this pamphlet is admitted I will show that Major Haller is its author and publisher or that he assisted in its preparations or publications.

'I introduce this pamphlet under the ruling of the court that no testimony of a date later than that of the dismissal of Major Haller should be admitted except in rebuttal. I offer this pamphlet in rebuttal.

'Major Haller has introduced testimony as to his general character for loyalty, this testimony covering a period of many years commencing before the war and extending beyond the time of his dismissal. In admitting testimony on the part of the petitioner of a date later than that of his dismissal I think that the court even omitting the exception in its ruling has opened the door widely to the admission of the like testimony referring to the same period. I offer this pamphlet however, under the exception in the ruling, in rebuttal of the testimony produced by the petitioner as to his general character for loyalty and I submit to the court that an officer's avowed opinions given when under the restraint of his oath and commission would not so truly indicate his sentiments of loyalty or disloyalty as utterances or writings of a period or when such restraint no longer exists. This pamphlet I will add was published in 1863 shortly after Major Haller's dismissal.'

The counsel for the petitioner said: 'I object to the introduction of this pamphlet for the reason that this court is authorized to inquire into the matter of the dismissal of Major Haller and is not justified in giving into his acts subsequent to the order of dismissal. The pamphlet that the Recorder propose to introduce is an act of Major Haller's subsequent to the date of his dismissal and therefore did not influence the mind of the Secretary of War or that of the President in ordering the dismissal and makes no part of the subject matter into which the court is authorized to inquire.'

The court was then cleared and after mature deliberation opened and the decision of the court announced by the Recorder, 'The court sustains the objection.'

The Recorder then offered in evidence "An affidavit of Major Granville O. Haller, dated August 8th 1841 attached to which is a pamphlet of 26 pages which Major Haller in the affidavit swears he complied and had printed in 1863." He then said 'The court has admitted testimony on the part of the petitioner showing his efforts to obtain a hearing, a trial or the means of publicly vindicating his character for loyalty. These are acts of the petitioner bearing upon his dismissal but not all of his acts. At the time that he was making these efforts he was also publishing this pamphlet. The acts and the publication are synchronous. As a part have been admitted I claim that all should be.'

The counsel for the petitioner said: 'I make the same objection to this paper as to the one just thrown out by the court. It is clearly not admissible for the official of the War Department could goad an officer into uttering or writing foolish things or even disloyal sentiments and then use these utterances or writings in justification of its illegal and oppressive acts that produce them.'

The court was then cleared and after mature deliberation opened and the decision of the court announced by the Recorder, 'That the court decides not to accept the paper.'

The Recorder then stated: 'I would like to offer in evidence several endorsements upon papers pertaining to this case and the report of Judge Advocate General Dunn of 1871. I offer these as so many decisions by competent authority as to the merits of the case and the loyalty or disloyalty of the toast proposed.

'To sustain my offer I will state that the petitioner has refused to certain attempts made by himself to effect restoration to rank. These attempts consisted, as he himself states, in the submission to the War Department at different times of written documents. As these documents have been referred to I claim that I have the right to introduce them and as I understand the petitioner's answer then I think that I have the right to introduce under cover of it all papers bearing upon his case which have been submitted by him or in his behalf to the War Department since his dismissal except such as the court has already rejected.

'As to the report of the Judge Advocate General Dunn it is a report made on a reference of the case to him and as such should have the same authority as similar experts in civil cases.'

The counsel for the petitioner said: 'I object to the introduction of the endorsements made by official or papers filed in the War Department asking leave for Haller to appear before a court martial. They have nothing to do with this question before the court.

The opinion of the Secretary of War or the Judge Advocate General as to the propriety of allowing Major Haller a court cannot be made evidence of Haller's acts or utterances of disloyalty prior to the date of the order of his dismissal. They may be are so sound as legal opinions or commendable as executive acts, but they are not evidence.'

The court was then cleared and after mature deliberation opened and the decision of the court announced by the Recorder: "That the court sustains the objection.'

The court then at 1.15 O'clock P.M. adjourned to meet tomorrow the 14 of May at 11 O'clock A.M.

SEVENTH DAY

Washington D.C.
No. 1700 Pennsylvania Avenue
May 14TH 1879

The court meet pursuant to adjournment at 11 O'clock A.M this day

Present
Lieutenant Colonel H. F. Clarke, Assistant Commissary General of Subsistence
Major John Hamilton, 1st Artillery
Major George G. Hunt, 1st Cavalry
2nd Lieutenant G.A. Postley, 3rd Artillery, Recorder

The Petitioner and his counsel were also present. The proceedings of the 13th instant were then read and approved.

The Recorder then offered in evidence the following disposition of General R. C. Schenck. The disposition was read by the Recorder down to and including the question 'Have you since that time had occasion to change your impressions, or have they since been confirmed. I refer to the time of the dismissal of Major Haller.'

The counsel for the petitioner objected to the question for the reason that 'General Schenck has already given all he know relative to the matter of the dismissal and no matter what occurred subsequent to the date of the dismissal (and that is all that General Schenck can have since learned to confirm the opinion he had of Major Haller in 1863) such acts cannot now he produced in evidence to justify the order of dismissal.'

The Recorder replied 'A similar question has been asked by the counsel for the petitioner in three different instances and has been admitted by the court. 1st in the testimony of Peter Bentz, viz: Question Have you ever known Major Haller guilty of any disloyal acts or expressions?

Answer: Never

Question: Was Major Haller noted for his disloyalty in York, Pennsylvania in 1862 or 1863 or since?

Answer: He was not so noted.

Again in the testimony of Colonel Levi Maish. The question was asked by the counsel for the petitioner: What was Major Haller's reputation in York, Pennsylvania, for loyalty during the war, and what is it now?

The counsel for the petitioner has introduced testimony to establish Major Haller's character for loyalty since 1863; I claim that I have the right to introduce testimony in rebuttal

The court was then cleared and after mature deliberation opened and the decision announced by the Recorder 'That the court has decided to admit the question'. The Recorder then concluded the reading of the deposition. The deposition was then accepted by the court.

CLOSING STATEMENTS

May it please the court: Confidently believing that he has clearly, distantly and fully disproved the charge of disloyal conduct and the utterance of disloyal sentiments upon which his dismissal was based Major Haller is not disposed to take up the time of the court by any discussion of the evidence before you. He will not comment on the conflicting statements in the evidence upon which the Secretary of War based his action in this case; nor on the insufficiency of that evidence though uncontradicted as a justification for inflicting upon an old soldier the severest punishment authorized by law or known to the service; nor will he attempt to rearrange the evidence that this inquiry has developed in vindication of his honor as a loyal, devoted, faithful soldier of the Government of the United States. You have given him an impartial, patient hearing; you are each of you as fully competent as any man he can bring here to weigh the evidence for and against him, and to give each item its true value and, therefore, he leaves the evidence for you to digest without any suggestions from anyone in his behalf.

There is, however, a question of law involved in his case, to which he wishes especially to direct your attention. This question lies at the foundation of the case before you; it is this: As the statue of July 17, 1862 granted to the President of the United States- and only to him- the power, in time of war, to dismiss any commissioned officer of the Army by his simple order and without assigning any reason; must the President exercise that power in person? Or was it intended by the legislator that the President could authorize the Secretary of War to exercise this power without consulting the President and securing his assent to each dismissal?

No one, I think, will question the statement that punishments cannot be inflicted upon the citizens of the United States who are in the military service of the Government except in pursuance of law- i.e. that no official of the U.S. has the legal power to invent new military offences, or to establish other modes of trying officers, or to declare men unfit for service in any other way than those laid down in the laws passed by Congress for the government of the Army and in the rules and regulations made in pursuance therefore; and especially that an officer cannot forfeit his honor or his life except to the written law and that such forfeiture cannot be enforced except by the official named in the law and in strict conformity to the mode laid down in the law. Nor can anyone doubt but that inasmuch as our President is the creature of our Constitution that he derives all of the power he possesses from the Constitution and the laws made in pursuance of the Constitution. There is no hereditary or divine right or prerogative about him; he is simply toe creature of a plainly written law and so long as he ahs the sanction of this law for his acts they are potential and conclusive but when he lacks such sanctions his act has no more legal force than the act of any other citizen.

This being fact and it also bring true that judges whether civil or military are bound to give a strict construction to all statues inflicting punishments –i.e. to require of all who enforce such statues a strict compliance with their requirements; I ask again must the President exercise this power of peremptory dismissal in person? It may be said that as this law authorizes the President to dismiss officers by his order as Commander in Chief he can issue such orders as all military orders are issues- i.e. over the signature of the Secretary of War who is the official through whom he issues all his commands to the Army. Admitting this, does it then follow that the Secretary of War has power to order the dismissal of officers 'By command of the President' that therefore he has power to authorize the Adjutant General to order the dismissal of an officer 'By the command of the Secretary of War"? If it does then the Adjutant General can pass a like authority over to his assistant and so on down until the power to affix for life the brand of dishonor on any soldier of the government is lodged in the hand of the humbled man in the Army. It is undoubtedly true that it is absurd to hold that the law in question authorized the handing over of this power from one to another as stated, but it is equally true that if the Secretary of War can place in the hands of an Inspector General power that he received from the President under the law in question then it logically follows that the Inspector General himself can turn it over to his next subordinate. But as this leads us to the absurdity I have pointed out we are forced to abandon the theory that because the Secretary of War may issue an order of peremptory dismissal 'By command of the Secretary of War.' This theory then is not correct; the law does not warrant anyone to issue an order 'By command of the Secretary of War' dismissing peremptory a commissioned officer of the Army. But the only authority the Adjutant General had for his Special Order No. 331, Series of 1862, was an endorsement on an old yellow envelop in the following words:

War Department, July 22, 1863
Major G.O. Haller, 7th Infantry, will be dismissed from the service of the US for disloyal conduct and the utterance of disloyal sentiments.
By order of the Secretary of War
James A. Hardie
Asst. Inspector General

This S.O. No. 331 was then not founded on such an order as the statue of July 17, 1862 directs shall be issued in such cases and it therefore did not dismiss Major Haller from the Army but he is today and has been continuously since 1839 in contemplation of the law, a commissioned officer of the Army and entitled to all the rights and privileges belonging to his commission.

Again: This act of July 17, 1862 authorizes the President to dismiss any officer that <u>he thinks</u> unfit for the military service. Now, unquestionably, the President must pass judgment upon each officer that is proposed to dismiss under this act before the dismissal can be made and it must appear of record in each case that the President did pass judgment. But the paper before you does not say, nor have we a right to infer from it, that President Lincoln ever passed judgment on Major Haller. On the contrary, Major Hardie, in his order direction the Adjutant General to the Army dismissing Major Haller, says that he gives this directions 'By order of the Secretary of War'- i.e. that the Secretary of War has passed judgment upon Major Haller.

It is true that the Adjutant General in his order says the dismissal is made by direction of the President, but this S.O. No. 331 is only one of the general forms of the Adjutant General's Office, that was used in announcing to the Army the fact that the President had dismissed the officer whose name appeared in it in the handwriting of some clerk. If the truth of the statement in this order is called in question as I now call in question the truth of the statement in War Department's S.O. No. 331 of 1863, the order itself does not prove that the President did in fact order the dismissal. If it could be held that the Adjutant General's orders be conclusive on that point it would place it in the power of the Adjutant General, at any time, of his own motion, to peremptorily dismiss officers in time of war and would deprive the dismissed officer of the right to show that the President did not order the dismissal and so you gentlemen would not hold your commissions during good behavior nor would you hold them as your commissions read 'at the pleasure of the President' but you would hold them at the pleasure of the Adjutant General. If this is the tenure by which you hold your commissions that fact has only recently been discovered and I will respectfully submit that it lessens materially not only the value but the dignity of your office.

But the trial is that special order of the Adjutant General does not prove that the President did direct the dismissal of the officers named therein; the fact of such dismissal is a separate and distinct fact from the Special Order of the Adjutant General announcing it. The President order is the <u>cause</u> and the Adjutant General's the <u>effect</u>- they cannot exchange places or be substituted for each other and therefore if an officer assents that the Adjutant General's order is not founded on an order of the President's the order of the President must be produced and if it cannot be the order of the Adjutant General is nugatory.

Now where is the order of the President directing the Adjutant General to issue S.O. No. 331 of 1863? The fact is there is no such order and there never was one and the War Department doesn't pretend that there ever had been- on the contrary, the Department informs you that S.O. No. 331 was issued in pursuance of the forgoing endorsement of General Hardie.

I must therefore ask that you will find on this point that Major Granville O. Haller was not dismissed the service of the U.S. 'By command of the President of the U.S' but 'By command of the Secretary of War' who had no authority to make such dismissal.

The Recorder replied as follows: The question of the legality of the dismissal of an officer such dismissal requiring the approval of the President and not being by his sign manual has frequently arisen and with a single exception, as far as I can learn, has been decided affirmatively.

The exception the decision of the President in the case of Major Runkle[69] – was rendered in opposition to the opinion of the Judge Advocate General and the Attorney General who held that the dismissal was in proper form.

In the case of Major Runkle the dismissal was authenticated by the Secretary of War- Secretary Belknap[70]- and the recent decision of the President was to the effect that the signature of the President was necessary. Similar cases have answer since which have been carried to the President who has uniformly refused to take any action in the matter.

The case of Major Runkle was brought up in the Senate, and the Judiciary Committee, with two dissenting voices, reported March 3rd 1879 that the President was using and that the dismissal of Major Runkle was in proper form. I will read that portion of the Report of the Committee which refers to the point at issue:

> The Committee are of the opinion that Benjamin P. Runkle was regularly tried and sentenced by the court martial named in the papers and that the sentence of the court was duly, effectually, regularly and legally approved by the President of

---

[69] Major Benjamin Runkle retired in 1870 and was dismissed from military service in 1873 on charges of embezzlement but was reinstated in 1877 by executive order of President Hayes. In 1887 the Supreme Court decided that he "was never legally cashiered or dismissed from the army" and was entitled to his back pay (RUNKLE v. U S, 122 U.S. 543)

[70] William Belknap, son of Maj. Belknap who was with Haller during the Seminole war; was appointed as Secretary of War by President Grant in 1869. Charged with accepting money in exchange for a military appointment and resigned from office; acquitted by the Senate on August 1, 1876

the United States was lawfully dismissed from the Army of the United States.

Now recently March 19th 1879, in the case of W.H. Campion, 1st Lieutenant 4th Infantry, the Attorney General decided that
> In the absence of any specified form, or mode for such action, prescribed in the statue on the subject (106 Article of War) the signing of the confirmation by the Secretary of War was a legal and sufficient mode of authenticating the decision and will of the President in the case; that the authentication of the Secretary is to be presumed, in the absence of evidence to the contrary to have been made wit the knowledge and by the direction of the President and that in this instance, as in the instance of other orders emanating from the Executive Department, the action of the Secretary is in the general contemplation of the law the action of the President.

This view has been frequently set forth by the Supreme Court and the Attorney General- Wilcox v. Jackson 13 Peters 498. US v. Eliason 16 Peters 302 and other cases. Opinions of Attorney General I, II 67, VI 326 587, VIII 453,473,725, IX 463, XIII 5, X 453. This has been the uniform practice.

Up to 1828 there is not a single instance of the dismissal of an officer by the sign manual of the President. In the above case of W. H. Campion the dismissal was authenticated by the Secretary of War but in the case of Paymaster Clark the Attorney General has gone a step further. He holds that even this is not necessary to give legality to a dismissal. In this case the dismissal was authenticated by the Adjutant General and the Attorney General held that the dismissal was in proper form, the authentication of the Secretary of War not being necessary, that of a staff officer being sufficient.

The counsel for the petitioner said: If the court please I desire to state in reply to the remarks of the Recorder that if the authorities referred to by the Recorder are to be allowed to have any bearing on this case that I am prepared to show that, prior to the War of the Rebellion, there were but three dismissals of commissioned officers of the Army, by sentence of court martial, in which the President did not sign the court martial record and further that there is no decision of the Supreme Court of the United States confirming the view that is competent for the Secretary of War to approve, or disapprove, a court martial record that contains a sentence of dismissal of a commissioned officer.

But the law and decisions relating to the approval or disapproval of a court martial record have no bearing upon the question of law I have presented to you in this case. The one is a judicial act, the other i.e. the dismissal by order of the President, is an executive act; and I have simply claimed in this case that the law of 1862 empowered the President to perform a certain executive act in cases that he alone has power to select and that even though it may be admissible for the Secretary of War to do this act by command of the President that it is not admissible for the Adjutant General, or any other person, to do the same act by command of the Secretary of War.

The court was then cleared for deliberation and having maturely considered the evidence address renders its findings and opinions as follows:

FINDINGS AND OPINIONS OF THE COURT

The accusation against Major G.O. Haller appears to be substantially thus: That on the evening of December 16th and 17th 1862 Haller, then a Major of the 7th U.S. Infantry, and commanding the Post Headquarters, Army of the Potomac, during a conversation with the then Lt. Commander C.H. Wells as to the conduct of the war did express in his tent at Falmouth, VA, before Fredericksburg certain so-called disloyal sentiments to wit.

First: That he Haller was particularly severe on the Administration for displacing Gen. McClellan, and was much excited at the Lt. Commander's dissenting from the declaration made by another army officer present; to this effect that Gen. McClellan was the only General that existed.

That on the reporting officer's (Lt. Commander Wells) remarking that he was astonished to hear such opinions (ones condemnatory of a paper money issue, given by the other army officer present) from a class of men whom he had always found loyal- he, Haller, said 'While we were together in York I did all I could to prepare you for what you would hear in the Army. I had noticed in my conversations with you that you were ultra in your opinions.'

That when the reporting officer determined to leave the tent by reason of the expressed disloyalty, Major Haller said, with considerable violence of manner, that if his presence was so disagreeable to the Lt. Commander he would procure a companion to share the tent with him- a black Republican- and he would go elsewhere.

And that the reporting officer had heard him, Haller, say that he considered the President responsible for the loss of life at Fredericksburg and that Haller had invariably denounced the conduct of the Administration to put down the Rebellion and the we would always fail unless Gen. McClellan should be restored to the command of the Army of the Potomac.

He, Haller, also took pleasure in speaking of acts of courtesy between officers of the United States and the Confederate Army. That in this tone he always spoken and said his intercourse with the Confederate officers had always been of the most agreeable nature.

He, Haller, denied that our prisoners at Richmond had been hardly treated.

Second: Haller is also charged by the reporting officer with having, on the same occasion, given the following toast 'Here's to a

Northern Confederation and a Southern one while Lincoln is President.'

The other Army officers present Major Whiting 5th Calvary, as well as the petitioner swear to the toast having been in these terms, 'Here's to the Constitution as it is and the Union as it was.'

Third: A charge volunteered by the Judge Advocate General, in a report July 9th 1863, to the Secretary of War was that Major Haller had not denied the charges made against him by Lt. Commander Wells.

Fourth: Section 17 Act of Congress approved July 17th 1862 reads as follows: 'And be it further enacted that the President of the United States be and hereby is authorized and requested to dismiss and discharge from the military service either in the Army, Navy, Marine Corps or volunteer force, in the United States service in his judgment either renders such officer unsuitable for or whose dismissal would promote the public service.'

The court is of the opinion that under the law the President was requested to dismiss or discharge any officer of the Army where dismission, in the President's judgment, would promote the public service.

According to this, a dismissal under this law would be legal should the President simply judge that he could find a better man for the place or that the place would be better void, but as the order sets forth the reason for dismission, disloyalty, it is fair to infer that but for conviction of disloyalty to the judgment of the President the officer would not have been dismissed.

The main point then to be considered by this court is, was Major Granville O. Haller's conduct disloyal before July 25, 1863 such as properly to convict him of disloyalty to the judgment of the President?

The court finds nothing disloyal in the sentiment expressed by Major Haller in the discussion of the conduct of the War. Many men fought loyalty for the Union of our country who did not approve the policy of the Government in the conduct of the War. Many had an extreme loyalty to their particular chief which, though probably lessening their usefulness, was not intended as a disloyalty to their country's unity. These expression of opinions were imprudent, injudicious and prejudicial and should have been restrained but when accompanied by loyal acts clearly free the utterer from the charge of disloyalty.

The court is of the opinion that Major Haller was right in not attempting a defense against the report of Lt. Commander Wells until the charge should be brought to this notice through the proper military channels.

As to the toast as charged the court finds it so unintelligible and as not representing any tone of political thought there known to its members, that it is more ready to believe the wording of the evidence adduced by the petitioner, 'Here's to the Constitution as it is and the Union as it was' rather than the untranslatable one charged.

The word 'conduct', in S.O. No. 331, appears by all the evidence adduced to be only sentiments expressed; no overt act of disloyalty is charged.

The Judge Advocate General's examination of Lt. Commander Wells was so ex parte in its character that it merely served to base charges upon and was not for the purpose of reaching the interval merits of the case.

This examination was then sent, July 9th 1863, to the General in Chief, and with true military propriety he recommended in forwarding it to the Secty of War, that Haller should be brought before a then existing court to be given the opportunity to disprove the charges. This court is of the opinion that non-conformity with this recommendation has not resulted in advantage to the Government nor in a public utterance of justice to the petitioner.

Therefore, in conformity with the Joint Resolution of Congress, approved March 3rd 1879, and Special Orders No. 80, dated Headquarters of the Army, Adjutant General's Office, Washington April 3, 1879, the court finds that Major Granville O. Haller, late 7th U.S. Infantry, was dismissed for disloyal conduct and disloyal sentiments on insufficient evidence- 'wrongfully'; and therefore, hereby, by virtue of the authority constituting it- does 'annul' said dismissal published in S.O. No. 331, dated War Department, A.G.O, Washington D.C July 25th 1863.

H.F. Clarke
Lt. Col AGCS, USA
Prest. of Court of Inquiry

There being no further business in the court at 3.15 P.M. adjourned "sine die"

H.F. Clarke
Lt. Col AGCS, USA
Prest. of Court of Inquiry

OPINIONS TO THE COURT OF INQUIRY

War Department
Bureau of Military Justice
May 20, 1879

Hon. Geo. W. McCrary[71]
Secretary of War

Sir:
    I have the honor to return herewith the proceedings transmitted to me yesterday for review of the Court of Inquiry convened by your direction in the case of Granville O. Haller, late Major and to remark as follows:
    The court in this case was assembled under the following Joint Resolution of Congress, approved March 3, 1879:
    Joint Resolution requiring the assembling of a court of inquiry in the case of Major Granville O. Haller, late of the Seventh Infantry United States Army.
    Resolved by the Senate and House of Representatives of the United States of America in Congress assembled, that the Secretary of War is hereby required to order a military court-martial or court of inquiry to inquire into the matter of the dismissal of Major Granville O. Haller, late of the Seventh Infantry, United States Army; said court to be fully empowered to confirm or annul the action of the War Department by which said Haller was summarily dismissed the service on or about the ninth of July, anno Domini eighteen hundred and sixty-three, said court to be assemble at such convenient place as may be designated by the President; and the findings to have the effect of restoring said Haller to his rank, with the promotion to which he would be entitled, if it be found that he was wrongfully dismissed, or to confirm his dismissal, if it be otherwise found. Said Haller shall notify the commanding officer of his readiness to appear before said court; and he shall have reasonable notice of the time of the assembling of the same: Provided, that said Haller shall

---

[71] George McCrary served as Secretary of War from 1877-79

receive no pay or allowances of any kind whatsoever for the time he was out of the service.

The only thing authorized or required by this Resolution to be done by the Secretary of War is to order the court. This has been done. The only thing authorized or required to be done by the President is to designate the place of the assembling of the court. This also has been done. All the rest of the power and authority conferred, or proposed to be conferred, by the statute is- in terms- conferred upon the court. This is 'fully empowered to confirm or annul' the summary dismissal of Haller and if it finds that he was 'wrongfully dismissed' its 'findings' are 'to have the effect of restoring him to his rank with the promotion to which he would be entitled 'had he remained continuously in office.'

Pursuant to this power the court of inquiry met and after hearing testimony came to the following finding: 'The court finds that Major Granville O. Haller, late 7th Infantry, was dismissed for disloyal conduct, and disloyal sentiments, on insufficient evidence- "wrongfully"; and therefore, hereby, by virtue of the authority constituting it- does "annul" said dismissal published in S.O. No. 331, dated War Department, A.G.O., Washington, D.C., July 25th, 1863.'

In regard to the merits of this case, I would remark that, upon the evidence introduced and admitted by the court, I should be inclined to the opinion that the punishment inflicted was a more severe one than was quite justified, even in time of war, by the nature of the offence committed.

But a full discussion of the testimony is deemed to be uncalled for, in view of the peculiar provisions of the Joint Resolution, and of the opinion entertained by me that the finding of the court cannot legally have the effect declares that it should have.

The Resolution, which clearly, (Lee XIV Opinions, 449) recognizes the fact that Major Haller was legally dismissed- a fact also found by the court and was thus a civilian at its date, does not, ads in usual in legislation looking to the restoration of dismissed officers, authorize the President to nominate to the Senate or reappoint the part. The statue, as worded, is not to be executed by the Executive, but is to execute itself. Ex proprio vigor, it is to restore the part to the Army through the action of a military court. But the Constitution (Art. II, Sec. 2, par. 2) provides that the President, in concurrence with the Senate, shall exercise the general appointing power of the Government; and that this power cannot be exercised independently by Congress in the case of an Army officer, so that its Act shall per se constitute his commission, is to clear for discussion. (Lee XIV Opinions of Attorney's General, 449) That Congress has not power to 'annul' a valid executive act is also obvious.

But it may possible be claimed that Congress, in empowering the court of inquiry to 'annul' the dismissal and in declaring that its finding shall have the effect of reinstating the party in officer, intended to exercise the discretionary power, conferred upon it by the Section of the Constitution above cited, of vesting in 'the courts of law,' (equally with 'the heads of departments') the appointment of 'inferior officers.' But, admitting that officers of the Army are 'inferior officers', in the sense in which the term is here employed, I am unable to find any authority for construing the words 'the courts of law' otherwise than as meaning the U.S. Judiciary as constituted and defined by Art. III, Sec. 1 of the Constitution. Atty. General Legare[72] (IV Opinion, 164) refers to these words as describing 'the judicial tribunals' of the United States. Atty. General Speed[73] (XI Opinions, 213) cites them as synonymous with 'the federal tribunals.' The authorities further refer to the power in question as vested in the courts for the purpose simply of providing themselves with the necessary ministerial officials. Thus Atty. General Akerman[74] says: 'Without efficient servitors, a court of law is impotent; therefore Congress may vest appointments in courts.' In ex parte Hennen, 13 Peters, 258, the Supreme Court observed: 'The appointing power here designated was no doubt intended to be exercised by the department of the government to which the officer to be appointed most appropriately belong. The appointment of clerks of courts properly belongs to the courts.' And Story (2 commentaries on the Constitution, §1536) remarks that the power has been exercised by Congress in giving to the courts 'the narrow prerogative of appointing their own clerk and reporter.' In view of these authorities it would certainly be preposterous to claim that Congress is authorized by the Constitution to empower military courts, which are no part of the Judiciary of the United States but merely instrumentalities of the executive power, to make appointments of officers of the Army.

---

[72] Hugh Legare, Second Attorney General under President Tyler
[73] James Speed, Last Attorney General under President Lincoln and first under Johnson
[74] Amos Akerman, Second Attorney General under President Grant

It may, however, further be claimed that this case comes within the ruling of Atty. General Williams[75] in the case of Von Leuttwitz, already referred to (XIV Opinions, 448). In this case an Act of Congress provided: 'The the Secretary of War be, and is hereby, directed to amend the record of the said A.H. Von Leuttwitz, so that he shall appear on the rolls and records of the Army for rank as if he had been continuously in service.' The Attorney General, in holding that no Act of Congress could of itself operate to appoint a civilian to a military office, yet goes on to say 'Considering the meaning of this act, rather than what it says, and the duty of the Executive to execute as far as practicable the will of Congress, no matter how inapposite the words in which it is expressed, my opinion is that the act under consideration confers upon the President the power to appoint Von Luettwitz a first lieutenant in the usual way.' This is the most extreme instance of a liberal construction of a statue in favor of the exercise of the executive power of appointment with which I am acquainted, and one which I can but regard as unsafe to follow. Its application, however, cannot be extended to the present case, since here, Congress not only specifically confines the power of the Secretary of War and the President to the ordering of the court to assemble at a designated place, but reserves, in express terms, to itself, or rather to the military court, the function of appointment. The President is, thus neither directly nor by implication authorized to exercise the appointing power but is distinctly excluded from such exercise. And, in the absence of special authority from Congress, he is not empowered to appoint a civilian to any army office of a grade higher than that of second lieutenant.

It is thus my conclusion that the Joint Resolution in the case of Haller has authorized his reinstatement or appointment by an agency not recognized by the Constitution and that the same must therefore be held, as had been held of other statutes in similar instances (see IV Opinions, 162; XI do., 209; XIII do; 516) to be unconstitutional and so wholly inoperative for the purpose for which it was designed.

If this opinion is concurred in, no action with a view to the rehabilitation or recognition of Haller as an officer of the Army, can, of course, be taken by the Executive. I would suggest however, that the Bureau be directed to furnish Mr. Haller with a copy of the proceedings and findings of the Court of Inquiry for such use as he

---

[75] George Williams, Third Attorney General under President Grant

may desire to make of the same in bringing his case before Congress or otherwise.

W.M. Dunn
Judge Advocate General

The Judge Advocate General, in returning the Record of the Court of Inquiry in this case to the Secretary of War, states that the Joint Resolution authorizing the creation of this court distributes the power that is to be exercised under it as follows:
1st- It confers upon the Secretary of War the power to order the court
2nd- It confers upon the President the power to say where the court shall be assemble, and
3rd- It confers upon the 'findings of the court' the power to restore Major Haller to the service
And he further says that inasmuch as the act authorizing the creation of the court 'recognized the fact that Major Haller was legally dismissed' and the further fact that the court found the same thing that therefore Major Haller was 'a civilian' at the date the Resolution was passed and approved.
For these reason he comes to the conclusion that the Resolution in question attempts to confer upon a military court the power to 'appoint a civilian' to a commission in the Army and is therefore an unconstitutional act and void.
To this opinion of the Judge Advocate General, Major Haller makes the following answer:

II

He says the question whether he was or was not legally dismissed the military service of the United States has never been passed upon by competent authority and that if it is eve decided that decision to have any force in law must be made by some judicial tribunal authorized by law to pass upon that question. That in no event is Congress competent to adjudicate that question and consequently if it be true that Congress has 'recognized' the fact that he was legally dismissed the service (when if fact he was not) such recognition would no more settle that question and so deprive him of the right to restoration tan the recognition of the fact that he was illegally dismissed would restore him a commission of which he had been legally deprived- i.e. it has not legitimate force either one way or the other.

I am entirely familiar wit the fact that the Chiefs of Bureau in the great Executive Departments have sometimes a profound respect for even the Resolutions of the Committees of Congress that express a doubt as to the legality or honesty of any matters with which they have to deal and are anxious but unable to reject under existing laws; but I am surprised to find that a prominent law officer of the Government would commit his Bureau to the statement that a mere 'suggestion' of Congress could legalize an illegal dismissal. This doctrine will not, of course, receive Executive sanction.

II II

He says that the Judge Advocate General is mistaken in saying that he court found the fact that he was legally dismissed the military service and he further says that inasmuch as the court was not authorized to find that fact any utterance of the court that would bear that interpretation would have no force.

The language of the court is as follows: 'The court finds that Major Granville O. Haller, late 7th Infantry was dismissed for disloyal conduct and disloyal sentiments on insufficient evidence, wrongfully.'

In this finding the court uses the language of the Adjutant General's order announcing the dismissal and the language of the statue under which it was assembled and has thereby consternated an awkward sentence which evidently means that it finds Major Haller was, on insufficient evidence, wrongfully dismissed the service. Now, the statue that authorizes the President to dismiss peremptorily any officer who, in his judgment, was unfit for the service does not authorize the Secretary of War, on insufficient evidence, to wrongfully dismiss a commissioned officer and consequently the meaning of the finding of the court is that the order of the Adjutant General announcing the dismissal of Major Haller was illegal and did not in fact dismiss him: and, therefore, it cannot be said that the court 'recognized' the fact that Haller was legally dismissed.

But the fact is the court was not authorized to find whether Major Haller was or was not dismissed the military service. The Act empowers it to inquire into the matter of the dismissal- i.e. into the charges on which the order announcing his dismissal was based all of which are matters of act not questions of law and it further directs that if the court finds that he was wrongfully dismissed- i.e. if it finds that the matters of fact charged against him were not true- to declare the same. So that even if the Record of the Court did show that the court recognized the fact that Major Haller was dismissed in 1863 it would be simply the private opinion of these officers, improperly placed in the Record of the Court, and would have no more weight than the same recognition by any other officers of the Army. The fact is the question as to the legality of Major Haller's dismissal has never been passed upon by anyone authorized to adjudicate that question and should that question ever be tried he is prepared to prove from the Records of the War Department to the satisfaction of any competent judge that President Lincoln did not order his dismissal- that therefore the Special Order of the War Department announcing his dismissal was illegally issued and consequently although he has for years been deprived of the command and pay to which he is entitled as a Major of Infantry still has not been dismissed from the military service of the United States.

    He therefore claims that he is not a civilian seeking an appointment but an officer of the Army demanding the recognition of this rights under his commission and that it was the recognition of this fact that moved Congress to pass and the President to approve the Joint Resolution of March 3, 1879 and not, as the Judge Advocate General assumes, the recognition of the fact that he had been legally dismissed.

III

    The Joint Resolution does not authorize the Court of Inquiry to appoint a civilian to a commission in the Army as asserted by the Judge Advocate General and is therefore not in violation of the Constitution.

    The strict construction of the letter of an Act of Congress that proposes to give a soldier of four wars a judicial investigation of charges that he claims were false and the avoidance of its spirit is not the character of construction that the law commands shall be made of any statutes and is especially obnoxious to the rule governing the interpretation of remedial statutes and yet such is the character of the construction that the Bureau of Military Justice in this case. Dwarrs says 'that a remedial act should be so construed as most effectually to meet the beneficial end in view and to prevent a failure of the remedy' and yet it appears that the Bureau has a mind, in this case, to reverse this old rule of construction by which the letter is made to give way to the spirit of the statute and in its place to order that, so far as this act is concerned the plain, unquestioned spirit of this statue together with the evident intent of the legislator shall be subordinated to the strict meaning of the words of the act which was evidently written by an unskilled hand.

> The statute in question is in the following words:
>> Joint Resolution requiring the assembling of a court of inquiry in the case of Major Granville O. Haller, late of the Seventh Infantry United States Army.
>> Resolved by the Senate and House of Representatives of the United States of America in Congress assembled, that the Secretary of War is hereby required to order a military court-martial or court of inquiry to inquire into the matter of the dismissal of Major Granville O. Haller, late of the Seventh Infantry, United States Army; said court to be fully empowered to confirm or annul the action of the War Department by which said Haller was summarily dismissed the service on or about the ninth of July, anno Domini eighteen hundred and sixty-three, said court to be assemble at such convenient place as may be designated by the President; and the findings to have the effect of restoring said Haller to his rank, with the promotion to which he would be entitled, if it be found that he was wrongfully dismissed, or to confirm his dismissal, if it be otherwise found. Said Haller shall notify the commanding officer of his readiness to appear before said court; and he shall have reasonable notice of the time of the assembling of the same: Provided, that said Haller shall receive no pay or allowances of any kind whatsoever for the time he was out of the service.

The records of the War Department show that Major Haller protested against his dismissal- denied that he had ever been guilty as charged and insisted upon a trial by court martial; that he exhausted all the means at his command to secure from the Executive branch of the Government a judicial determination of the charges against him and that having failed he at least appealed to Congress not for an appointment but for the right to defend himself against the charges upon which the order announcing his dismissal was based and in compliance with his petition Congress passed and the President approved the foregoing Act which grants him a trial by a military court. This Act empowers the military court to pass upon the question of his guilt or innocence of the specific charges brought against him in 1863 and directs it to make a finding of 'wrongfully dismissed' or 'rightfully dismissed' and it declares that the finding shall have the effect of annulling the order of dismissal or, of confirming it, as the case might be.

The proceedings of military court usually terminate with certain findings and a sentence based upon them; but in this case there was no sentence to be pronounced for it the court should find Major Haller rightfully dismissed there was the end of the case and there was no sentence for it to pronounce, and, on the other hand, if the court found that he was wrongfully dismissed there could of course be no sentence pronounced against him and consequently Congress had to give the findings in this case the force that the general law gives to the sentence of the military court; for, otherwise, the Act would have authorized a trial of the charges, but would not have authorized the delivery of a judgment or its execution. The case was a peculiar one- the court was authorized to find that Major Haller was wrongfully or rightfully dismissed and it was authorized to confirm or annul the action of the War Department. It is evident that the 'findings' of the court under this Act are to be accepted as the legal termination of the duties imposed upon the officers who were detailed to compose the court; these 'findings' like the findings in all military courts was to be the judgment, and in addition to this, these 'findings' are to stand in the place of the 'sentence' of the ordinary court.

The military court authorized by this Act differs, then, from other military courts only in the fact that its findings are to be executed without the court itself directing, by a formal sentence, the particular act or thing to be done in consequence of the finding, and this is due to the fact that the Act in question declares what shall be the effect of a finding of wrongfully or rightfully dismissed. But because the Act of Congress, in authorizing the creation of a special court to try an exceptional case, declares what the effect of a given finding shall be, in place of leaving it to the court to make this declaration in a formal sentence, it does not therefore follow that these findings have any more power than the sentence of a court would have, nor does it by any means follow that these findings are complete and perfect judgments in themselves conclusive on all concerned. On the contrary, as these findings are after all only the findings of a military court, this is to be conducted under the laws regulation all military trials, it follows that they like the sentence of other military court, have no vitality until they are approved by the President, who, the law says, is the only competent authority to approve the proceedings, findings and sentence of a court that could deprive an officer of the Army of his commission.

The obfuscation consequent on the power given to the 'findings' in this Act will pass away if we substitute for it the word 'sentence. The Act would then read as follows:

> The Secretary of War is hereby required to order a military court marital or court of inquiry to inquire into the matter of the dismissal of Major Granville O. Haller, late of the 7th Infantry, U.S. Army; said court to be fully empowered to pass a sentence annulling or confirming the action of the War Department by which said Haller was summarily dismissed the service on or about the 9 of July A.D. 1863, said court to assemble at such convenient place as may be designated by the President and the sentence to have the effect of restoring said Haller to his rank, with the promotion to which he would be entitled, if it be found that he was wrongfully dismissed or to confirm his dismissal if it be otherwise found,' etc.

This amendment would not change the meaning of the Act in the slightest particular. Its meaning is the same and the power it grants to the court is the same as that of the original Act and yet no man who is at all conversant with the general laws governing our Army will say that this Act gives the commissioned officers of the Army who are detailed to try the case the power to appoint, of their own motion and without the concurrence of the Chief Executive, a civilian to a commission in the Army. For the proceedings of this court would have to be conducted in accordance with the laws governing trials by court martial and these laws declare that a sentence such as is provided for in this Act shall not be carried into effect until the proceedings, findings and sentence of the court have been approved by the President of the United States.

The same law governs the Executive in executing the Act as it stands. A military court has been assembled, in pursuance of a special act, for the trial of charges against Major Haller, it was organized and it conducted all of its proceedings in strict accordance with the general statutes regulating the proceedings of military courts; it has made up its record, and the case has gone to the Secretary of War for the action of the President and here the matters rest. The commissioned officers of the Army composing the court have discharged their full duty, under the Act, they have found and properly too (for it is a disgrace upon the Department of War that such an officer, guilty of absolutely no offence against the Government, but loaded with long years of faithful service in its defense, should have been so dealt with), that Major Haller was wrongfully dismissed, on insufficient evidence, and they have declared Special Order No. 331 of 1863 annulled and yet Major Haller is not recognized and paid as an officer of the Army. The Judge Advocate General is mistaken then when he says: 'The statute, as worded, is not to be executed by the Executive but is to execute itself.'

All the proceedings under this statute, like the proceedings of any other military court in time of peace that affect the commission of an officer of the Army, are as dead as a hammer and will remain so until 'the proper reviewing authority'-i.e. the President of the United States- reviews and approves the proceedings and findings. And if the President should disapprove them, which he has the power to do, and should do if the proceedings are fatally irregular, or, the finding, in his opinion, not justified by the evidence this Act would be fully and completely executed and still Granville O. Haller would not be an officer of the Army. No man competent to judge this question can doubt this. The proceedings of the court have no vitality- the question of the wrongful or rightful dismissal of Major Granville O. Haller is not decided until the President has acted on this case and consequently the Act in question does not give the commissioned officers of the Army the power to 'appoint a civilian to a commission in the Army.' The Act, then, is not unconstitutional.

It will be observed that, under the law governing military trials, the President is fee to approve or disapprove the findings of this court. It is true that he could not appoint Haller to be Major of Infantry in the Army unless it be on a finding of 'wrongfully dismissed' by a military court under this particular Act, but that fact does not derogate from his constitutional powers, for neither the Constitution nor any statue gives him the power to appoint Major Haller, or any other person as Major of Infantry in the Army as it now stands. Nor is the fact that the President's powers to order the restoration of Granville O. Haller's name to the list Majors of Infantry is dependent upon a particular finding of a military court in derogation of the President's constitutional power to appoint men to commissions in the Army and such would not be the case even if Haller were in fact a civilian; for the authority referred to by the Judge

Advocate General in his opinion holds that 'notwithstanding that the appointing power alone can designate an individual fro an officer still either Congress, by direct legislation, or the President, by authority derived from Congress, can prescribe qualifications and require that the designation shall be out of a class of persons ascertained by proper tests to have those qualification.' (See Opin. XIII, p.576)

In this case Congress has simply provided by Joint Resolution that Major Haller's claim to 'the commission of Major of Infantry shall be tried or tested in the way in which all such cases are tested and if he is found worthy that he shall be restored.'

In the case of Von Luettwitz, the Attorney General declares that although the act for his relief provided only for the obliteration from the records of the Army of any entry or statement showing that he had been cashiered, making no provision for his restoration or re-appointment, and that there is no question but that he had been legally cashiered and was therefore in fact and truth a civilian at the date of the passage of the act, still he say: 'The manifest intent of Congress was that Von Luettwitz should be restored to the rank which he formally held in the Army, with pay to commence at the passage of the act.' Congress could not have intended that 'a vacancy should occur in the ordinary way before this was done, as the act contemplates that he shall be at once in service and receive pay from the time of its passage.

'Considering the meaning of this act rather than what it says, and the duty of the Executive to execute as far as practicable the will of Congress, no matter how inapposite the words in which it is expressed, my opinion is that the act under consideration confers upon the President the power to appoint Von Luettwitz a lieutenant in the usual way, with pay to commence from the 23rd of June, 1874' (Vol. XIV, p.449).

If we follow the opinion of the Attorney General in this case- and it is certainly more in accord with the rule for the interpretation of remedial statutes than the strict adherence to the cold letter of the law, that is insisted upon by the Judge Advocate General- we will find no trouble in executing the Act of Congress in Major Haller's case.

But the fact that the construction given by the Judge Advocate General to this Act is erroneous is established beyond controversy by the fact that it would annul the Act; which of itself proves his construction to be erroneous. On this point attention is called to the Opinion of Attorney General Legare in 4 Opinion, p. 164 where he says: 'Congress has power to vest the appointments of these inferior officers in the heads of departments. It has not power to vest it in collectors. Therefore the law, if it meant that, would be void. Therefore, again, the law must not be interpreted to mean that, if it can be interpreted to mean anything else. Then, is it susceptible of any other interpretation? Clearly, as Mr. Wert shows, it may very well mean that the nomination of each particular inspector, &c., shall be approved by the Secretary of Treasury.'

And another Attorney General says on this same point: 'That repeal Congress of course, was entirely competent to effect. The law, therefore, has established an office, and not designated any competent public authority as authorized to appoint the officer. On whom then devolves the power of filling the office?

'I am of the opinion that the President is by the Constitution vested with authority to appoint assistant assessors under the existing circumstances. The Constitution confers on the President the power to nominate and by and with the advice of the Senate to appoint all officers of the United States whose appointments are not in the interment otherwise provided for and whose offices shall be established by law. In the case of inferior officers Congress may provide for their appointment by the President alone the heads of departments or the federal tribunals. When Congress creates such offices and omits to provide for appointments to them, or provides in an unconstitutional way for such appointment the officers of the United States whose appointments are not therein otherwise provided for. The power of appointing such officers devolves on the President' (Vol. XI, p.213).

Before concluding my remarks on the construction given by the Bureau of Military Justice to Haller Joint Resolution I will call attention to the Act of March 3, 1865 which has been carried into Section 1230 of the Revised Statues of the United States. This general law is in the following words:

> In case any officer of the military or naval service who may be hereafter dismissed by authority of the President shall make an application in writing for a trial, setting forth under oath that he had been wrongfully and unjustly dismissed, the President shall, as soon as the necessities of the public service may permit, convene a court-martial to try such officer on the charges on which he was dismissed. And if such court-martial shall not award dismissal or death as the punishment of such officer, the order of dismissal shall be void. And if the court-martial aforesaid shall not be convened for the trial of such

officer within six months from the presentation of his application for trial, the sentence of dismissal shall be void.

That the power conferred on military courts by this Act is identical is identical with that conferred by the Haller Joint Resolution is apparent but this Act goes beyond the Haller Resolution in that the Act itself, without the intervention of a military court in given contingencies, revokes orders of dismissal- the legal as well as the illegal orders- and restores both the rightfully and the wrongfully dismissed officers.

In dealing with this Act the Bureau of Military Justice has not raised the question of its constitutionality but has uniformly treated it as a valid statute.

In one of many decisions of the Judge Advocate General in cases arising under this Act, he says: 'Where an officer who has been summarily dismissed is tried by court-martial under this act and acquitted his dismissal is thereby made void ab initis, and his statutes in the service is the same as if he had never been dismissed at all' (Digest Opin: JAG, Dismissal III, 5, page 151).

In consideration of the foregoing reasons Major Haller respectfully asks that the President of the United States grant him a review of the record of the proceedings of the military court in his case, to end that the law passed by Congress and approved by the President for his relief shall have the full force and effect intended it should have and a proper construction of the same must give.

Charles Ewing
Counsel for Major Haller

Executive Mansion
Washington, June 14, 1879

The foregoing proceedings and findings of the Court of Inquiry in the case of Major Granville O. Haller are approved; but the question as to the legal effect of the findings of said court and the approval thereof is reserved for consideration and decision hereafter by the proper authority and no order restoring him to the Army will be made until that question is determined.

R.B. Hayes[76]

June 21, 1879
To the Senate of the United States

    To carry out the effect of the findings of a Court of Inquiry accorded in conformity with the provision of the Joint Resolution of Congress approved March 3, 1879 entitled: "Joint Resolution convening the assembly of a Court of Inquiry in the case of Major Granville O. Haller, late of the Seventh Infantry- United States Army." I nominate the said Granville O. Haller for the appointment of Colonel of Infantry in the Army of the United States to rank from February 19, 1873 that being the rank he would have attained had he remained continuously in the service.

---

[76] Rutherford Hays, President of the United States

AFTER THE COURT OF INQUIRY

Washington City, DC
July 1st, 1879

Genl. E.D. Townsend
Adjutant General, U.S. Army

Sir,

    I have the honor to acknowledge the receipt, this day, of my commission of Colonel in the military service of the U.S. which, I hereby accept.
    I was born in York, York County, Pennsylvania, January 31st 1819 and am consequently sixty years and five months old.
    My residence for the past fifteen years has been Whidbey Island, Washington Territory.

Very respectfully,
Your obedt. servant
Granville Own Haller
Colonel of U.S Infy

Washington City, DC
July 2nd, 1879

Hon. Geo. W. Mclerany
Secy of War

Sir,
    Having received a commission from the United States as Colonel of Infantry, I have the honor to apply for orders to report to Brevet Major Genl. O.O. Howard, comd'y Department of the Columbia, to await further orders.
    I make this request for the reason that during the sixteen years I was deprived of my place in the Army of the U.S., by War Department Specl. Orders No. 331, Series of 1863, I was engaged in civil pursuits in Washington Territory and having left my business promptly on the receipt of the telegram from the Adjutant General,

USA, directing me to appear before the military court which assembled in this city on the 5th day of May last, for the trial of my case, I feel that I am justified in asking that I may be ordered to await assignment to duty in the locality in which it will be possible for me to oversee the settlement of the complicated business affairs which I left so hurriedly.

And further, as the question of the exact date as which my pay allowance in the army commences, must be determined by you, I have the honor to ask that you will notify the Paymaster General of the Army, that my pay commences on the 14th June 1879. My reason for asking pay from this time is the fact that on the 14th of June last the President approved the finding of the military court in my case that this approval of the President annulled the order of the War Department which alone deprived me of the command and pay due me as a commissioned officer of the U.S. Army and the joint resolution in pursuance of which my rights as a commissioned officer have been restored to me, declares that this annulment shall have the effect of restoring to me all my rights as an officer except the pay due me from the date of Specl. Order No. 331 up to the date of its annulment.

I have the honor to be
very respectfully,
Your obedt. servt.
Granville O. Haller
Colonel U.S. Infantry

Headquarters of the Army
Adjutant General's Office
Washington
July 3, 1869

Special Order No. 156
Extract

II. By direction of the Secretary of War, Colonel Granville O. Haller, U.S. Army, having reported to the War Department for duty will report to the Commanding General Department of the Columbia and there await further orders.

By command of General Sherman

Headquarters Department of the Columbia
Vancouver Barracks, W.T.
July 19, 1879

Special Orders No. 91

    1. Colonel Granville O. Haller, U.S. Army, having reported at these Headquarters, pursuant to orders from the War Department, will proceed to Coupeville, W.T. and there await further orders.

By command of Brigadier-General Howard
O.D. Greene,
Assistant Adjutant General

Headquarters Department of the Columbia
Vancouver Barracks, W.T.
September 8 1879
Special Orders No. 117
Extract

    2. Colonel Granville O. Haller, U.S. Infantry, (unassigned) will proceed to, and assume command of Fort Townsend, W.T.

By command of Brigadier-General Howard
O.D. Greene,
Assistant Adjutant General

Hdqrs. Mil. Div. of the Pacific & Dept. of California
Presidio of San Francisco, Cal.
September 18th 1879

Adjutant General, Washington DC

Do I understand that is the wish of the War Department to have Colonel G.O. Haller, assigned to duty in command of troops in the Department of the Columbia.

McDowell
Major General

War Dept, AGO
December 3, 1879

Shall Col. Haller be assigned to the vacancy made by the death of Col. Jeff C. Davis 23d Infantry. The law does not absolutely require his assignment to a regiment in terms but it was no doubt the intention to do so.

[no name given]

Headquarters of the Army
Washington DC
December 8, 1879

Respectfully submitted to the Hon. Sec. of War with the opinion that there is no escape from the conclusion that Colonel Haller must be promoted to the vacancy in the 23rd Infantry vice Davis and ordered to join his regiment.

W.T. Sherman
General

December 10, 1879[77]

The Secretary of War directs the assignment of Col. Haller as Col. 23d Inf vice J.C. Davis

E. D. Townsend
Adjt. Genl

---

[77] Haller commanded the 23rd Infantry until his retirement on February 6, 1882

Headquarters Department of the Missouri
Assistant Adjutant-General's Office
Fort Leavenworth, Kansas

February 2, 1880

Special Orders No. 24
Extract

1. Colonel Granville O. Haller, 23d Infantry, having reported at these Headquarters, in compliance with paragraph 5 of Special Orders No. 279, series of 1879, Adjutant-General's Office, will proceed to Fort Supply, I.T., and assume command of that post and of his regiment.
2. The Headquarters 23d Infantry are returned to Fort Supply, I.T. The Regiment Adjutant and his clerks will proceed there from the Cantonment on the North Forth of the Canadian River, I.T., with the regimental books and papers.

By command of Brigadier-General Pope

E.R. Platt,
Assistant Adjutant-General

After retiring from military service Haller moved his family to Seattle and became one of the prominent families in the region. The house where he and his family once resided, called Castlemont and located on Seattle's Capital Hill, was torn down because it could not keep up with modern technology of the time. The lot has been turned into a parking lot.

Western Union Telegraph Company
Seattle Washn May 3rd[78]
Adjt General
Washington DC

Colonel Granville O. Haller U-S-A retired died at his home here at five minutes past eight PM yesterday of Lagrippe[79],[80].

---

[78] 1897; Haller left behind his wife and two children

Robinson Asst Quartermaster.

---

[79] A type of influenza; epidemic catarrhal fever
[80] Haller, and his family, are buried at the Lakeview Cemetery in Seattle

COURT EXHIBIT A

Navy Yard
Phila- February 17th, 1863

Major Haller, U.S.A

My dear sir:

Since I wrote you in reply to your letter I have thought so much over what had occurred in your tent and which was the cause of my leaving you that I cannot se why I should not report your disloyal language to the Secretary of War, painful as it may be, but in these times when we are engaged in a deadly struggle to sustain our government I would sacrifice my son.

You uttered this expression in my presence 'Here's to a Northern Confederation and a Southern one while Lincoln is President' which you gave as a toast to Major Whiting in your tent, and, had also said, 'that you considered the President responsible for the loss of life at the battle of Fredericksburg.'

No one can doubt my loyalty, and, I hope you will give me the credit of performing my duty conscientiously.

I am, yours
C.H. Wells
Lieut. Commander
U.S.N.

COURT EXHIBIT B

Extract of a letter from Major G.O. Haller dated Jany. 10th 1863

I see that your remarks lead you to think that I entertain sentiments which ought not to be spoken openly. I have but one opinion, which I never hesitate to speak out, if I go into argument at all, and these I would present to our President, as Paul did, his belief, before the Chief Magistrate Felix.

York Penna Feby. 18th 1863
Lieut Commdr. C.H. Wells, U.S.N.
Comdg. Navy Yard, Phila

My dear sir,

Your letters of the 16th January and 17th February are received and contents noticed.

The absence of Major Whiting U.S.A. on a court martial at the City of Washington prevented any laying before him the former of the two letters and getting from him a denial of the statements which you make and then replying to yours.

I shall not ask you to take my won statements. Fortunately there was a witness present, on the occasion of the conversation referred to in your letters, who saw all, heard all, and knows all that occurred. I have not seen him since the receipt of your letters, but, I think whom called on he will give a statement which will remove the hallucination under which you seem to be laboring.

One thing I remember and I can hardly think that you have forgotten it. I gave the toast and only one it was 'The Constitution as it is. The Union as it was.'

If this is disloyalty then as Patrick Henry says: 'Make the most of it!'

In the frame of mind in which you have written it is obvious that all previous relations, however agreeable, are ignored. I shall not therefore trouble you with an account of your friends, nor the on dibs of this place.

As a Mason it is my duty to respect you as a Brother, but I trust you will so conduct your course towards all brethren, that

discord may not be charged upon you- harmony being the strength of all relationships, more especially this of ours.
    Fraternally yours,
    G.O. Haller

DEPOSITION OF GENERAL ROBERT C. SCHENCK

Deposition of General R.C. Schenck taken at his residence, 1344 Mass. Avenue, on the 13th of May 1879. to be made in evidence in the case of Major G.O. Haller, before a Court of Inquiry, convened by S O No. 80, dated Headquarters of the Army A.G.O, Washington, April 3, 1879, this deposition being taken by the Recorder in the presence of the petitioner and his counsel.

Question by Recorder: What is your name and present occupation and what position have you held in the military service.

Answer: Robert C. Schenck. I was last in public service as Minister of the United States to Great Britain, and during the Rebellion, up to December 1863, was in the military service of the United States. During the last year that I was in the service I was as Major General of Volunteers in command of the 8th Army Corps and the Middle Department, with my Hd Qts at Baltimore Md.

Question: Do you know of Major Haller of the 7 Inf who was dismissed in 1863 for disloyalty.

Answer: My recollections of Major Haller, or about him is indistinct; I doubt if until this moment I ever met him in person. I remember that he was ordered to my command on some duty but he probably reported to somebody on my staff.

Question: What was Major Haller's reputation for loyalty at that time?

Answer: I can't say that. I knew what his general reputation for loyalty was. I remember that Gov. Bradford of Maryland, for whose service, or benefit, in that state in some way he was ordered there, made objections, which he expressed to me, that Major Haller was not the kind of man he wanted and perhaps Gov. Bradford and others spoke of Major Haller as in their opinion sympathized too much with the Rebellion. This impression was created on my mind at the time by conversations with Bradford and others, but I recall no facts stating that connection, nor have I any personal knowledge that such exception to Major Haller was well founded. These rumors did create an unfavorable impression on my mind as to the extent to which I might rely on Major Haller's strict loyalty.

Question: Have you since that time had occasion to change your impressions or have they since been confirmed. I refer to the time of dismissal of Major Haller.

Answer: Nothing has occurred that I can recall, since the dismissal of Major Haller, to change my impression of his case, prior to or at the time of his dismissal, or to confirm any opinion I may then have formed except, that I was unfavorably impressed, and made to think that his dismissal was not without good cause, by the production to come and submission to me to be made of a printed pamphlet, which purported to be published, perhaps about 1863, by the Major, in reply to the charges made against him by Captain Wells of the Navy. This pamphlet was shown to me by some friends of Major Haller, on or more of the from Washington Territory, but not intended, on their part, to prejudice the case of Major Haller, though it had that effect on my mind.

CROSS EXAMINATION

Question by the Petitioner: Who first informed you that Haller was not a strictly loyal man

Answer: I can not tell. What I have referred to has been the first impression created by conversation or rumors about that which I remember distinctly is the charge which was made against him by Captain Wells of the Navy,- that he had given in his presence a disloyal toast, and was a sympathizer with the Rebellion- I have not a very clear recollection now of the circumstances attending the making of this charge, but I think Capt. Wells forwarded it to me in a letter and that I felt it my duty to communicate it, and did communicate it, to Mr. Stanton, the Sect'y of War. My impression is that I must have accompanied that communication of the charges by some letter, or comments of my own, but I can not remember distinctly.

Robert Schenck

COURT EXHIBIT F[81]

War Department
Washington City
June 6th 1863

Hon. Gideon Wells
Secretary of the Navy

    Sir:
    I have the honor to request that Lieutenant Commander C.H. Wells U.S. Navy be ordered to report in person in this city to Colonel Joseph Holt, Judge Advocate General of the Army to give evidence on charges made against an officer of the Army. His presence here would probably not be required for a longer period than one day.
    Col. J. Holt will inform you when it will be most convenient for him to see Commander Wells.

    I am, sir
    Very Respectfully
    Your obdt. Servant
    Edwin M. Stanton
    Secretary of War

Navy Department
June 9, 1863

    Sir[82],
    When summoned by Colonel Joseph Holt, Judge Advocate General of the Army, you will proceed to Washington D.C. without delay and report in person to that officer.
    You will forward a copy of this order to Colonel Holt.

    Very Respectfully
    Gideon Wells
    Secretary of the Navy

---

[81] Court exhibits c, d, and e have not been found
[82] Letter written to Clark Wells

U.S. Navy Yard
Philadelphia
June 19th 1863

    Sir,
    Agreeably to an order of the Secretary of the Navy, I herewith enclose to you a copy of a letter which I received from him this morning.

    I am very respectfully,
    Your obdt. Servant
    C.H. Wells
    Lieut. Commander
    U.S.N.
Col. Joseph Holt
Judge Advocate General of the Army
Washington City D.C.

DEPOSITION OF CLARK H. WELLS

The Deposition of Lieut. Commander C.H. Wells, U.S. Navy taken at the Office of the Judge Advocate General, July 9 1863, to be read as evidence in relation to certain charges of disloyalty preferred against Major Granville O. Haller U.S. Army.

The witness having been first fully sworn deposes as follows to wit:

Question by the Judge Advocate General: Are you acquainted with Major Granville O. Haller U.S. Army and if so how long and how intimately have you known him?

Answer: My first acquaintance with him was in 1861, the latter part of that year and became quite intimate with him the later part of 1862. There is also a family connection with him.

Question: What is his reputation if known to you in or out of the military service for loyalty or disloyalty?

Answer: I don't know what his reputation is for loyalty or disloyalty in the Army. But out of the army, particularly where he resides, York Penna, he is noted for his disloyalty. His brother-in-law, Edward Hersh, would testify to that.

Question: Did you or did you not on the 16th of September 1862 visit Major O. Haller in his tent opposite Fredericksburg VA!

Answer: I accompanied Major O. Haller from York Penna to opposite Fredericksburg VA in Dec 1862. We arrive there the day on the evening of the day on which the town was bombarded and the bridges thrown across; on that evening I was with him in his tent and remained with him two days after the battle of Fredericksburg.

Question: Please state if on the occasion referred to Major O. Haller expressed any sentiments in reference to the existing rebellion if so what were they and how were they expressed.

Answer: At the time referred to there were some half dozen, mostly junior officers in his tent, when the conversation took a general turn until late on the evening when there was by one officer besides Major O. Haller and myself present and that officer was Major Whiting. The conversation then partook of apolitical character, with reference to the prosecution of the war. Major. O. Haller was particularly server upon the Administration for displacing Genl McClellan in which Major Whiting agreed with him.

I took the ground that there were other generals as competent to lead the Army of the Potomac as Genl McClellan. Major Whiting replied that God Almighty had made but one general in our country to command and that was Gen. McClellan. Major O. Haller and Major Whiting were much excited at my expressing the opposite opinion. Major Whiting also denounced the Administration for printing paper money declaring it to be a fraud and illegal. I expressed my astonishment to both of these officers that they should talk in the way in which they did and that I was not prepared to hear army officers exposes themselves so and that in intercourse with them heretofore I had always found them to be loyal, having been associated with them on duty. Major Haller replied that while we were together in York he had done all he could to prepare me for what I would hear in the Army- that he had noticed in his conversations with me that I was ultra in my opinions. He then gave as a toast to Major Whiting 'Here's to a Northern Confederation and a Southern one while Lincoln is President.'- I then declared my intention of leaving his tent immediately in consequence of his disloyal language. He replied with considerable violence of manner that if his presence was so disagreeable to me he would procure a companion to share with me his tent- a black Republican and he would go elsewhere.

    Major Whiting deprecated this conduct and I said that he did not wish me to leave Major O. Haller's tent under such circumstances and had not been aware that I was an officer of the Navy. I replied that nothing would induce me to remain with Major O. Haller a moment longer even if I had to sleep in the open air. Major Whiting then invited me to his tent. Major O. Haller expressed regret that I should leave him in that abrupt way and that he would write to my father-in-law Henry Welsh of York all about the matter. I told him that he could do so as soon as he pleased. I passed that night with Major Whiting who expressed his regret in the morning at what had occurred in Major O. Haller's tent and when I asked Major Whiting if he recollected everything that had taken place in Major O. Haller's tent he said he didn't recollect all. That morning I called to see Major O. Haller to bid him good bye- we shook hands and he seemed to regret that I was about leaving him, remarking that what he had said that night he wished me distinctly to understand he would tell the President of the U. States. I replied that I wouldn't discuss any such matter with him. I then left and joined Gen. Franklin.

    Question: What did Major O. Haller say to you if any thing in regard to the responsibility which he believed rested on the President for the loss of life that occurred at the battle of Fredericksburg fought under Gen. Burnside.

Answer: I heard him say after the battle that he considered the President responsible for the loss of life at the battle of Fredericksburg.

Question: Have you had repeated conversations with Major O. Haller in reference to the Rebellion and the conduct of the War for its suppression; if so state what has been their general or invariable tone on his part.

Answer: He invariably denounced and criticized the conduct of the Administration to put down the Rebellion and that we would always fail unless Gen. McClellan should be restored to the command of the Army of the Potomac.

He also took pleasure in speaking of acts of courtesy between the officers of the U.S. Army and the Confederate Army. In this tone he always spoke and said his intercourse with the Confederate officers had always been of the most agreeable nature. He denied that our prisoners at Richmond had been harshly treated.

C.H. Wells
Lieut Commander, U.S.N.

BIBLIOGRAPHY

Bird, Anne, *Boise, The Peace Valley*. Caldwell, ID: The Caxton Printers, 1934.

Grant, Frederic James, *History of Seattle Washington with illustrations and biographical sketches of some of its prominent men and pioneers*. New York: American Publishing and Engraving, 1891.

Haller, Granville, *The Dismissal of Major Granville O. Haller of the Regular Army of the United States by order of the Secretary of War in Special Orders, No. 331, of July 25th, 1863*. Paterson, NJ: The Daily Guardian Office, 1863.

Hemphill, John, *West Pointers and Early Washington: The Contribution of U.S. Military Academy Graduates to the Development of the Washington Territory, from the Oregon Trail to the Civil War 1834-1862*. Seattle: The West Point Society of Puget Sound, Inc., 1992.

Letters Received by the Commission Branch of the Adjutant General's Office, 1863-1870, microfilm publication M-1064, roll 402. National Archives Building, Washington, DC.

Murry, Keith, *The Pig War*. Tacoma, WA: The Washington State Historical Society, 1968.

Rodenbough, Theodore, *The Army of the United States: Historical sketches of staff and line with portraits of general-in-chief*. New York: Maynard, Merrill & Co., 1896

Records Group 153, US Army Court of Inquiry, QQ-1133, Major G.O. Haller, 16W3/16/29/4/box 3288. National Archives Building, Washington, DC.

Schlicke, Carl, "Long Road to Vindication for Accused Northwest Soldier," *Columbia*, Vol. 1, No. 1 (Summer 1988), 21-29

Series of Haller Family letters, 1853-1859. Island County (WA) Historical Society, transcribed by Dr. Martin Chamberlain, 1989.

State of Pennsylvania, *Resolutions No. 11, Relative to the officers of the army of the United States, native or citizens of Pennsylvania, who distinguished themselves in the late war with Mexico*, 1849.

US House of Representatives, *The Committee on Military Affairs, to whom was referred the joint resolution (H.Res. 63) authorizing a court of inquiry in the case of Granville O. Haller, late of the Seventh Infantry, United States Army, having had the same under consideration, beg leave to submit the following report:*, 45th Congress, 2nd Session, Report No. 375.

US Congress, *Joint Resolution requiring the assembling of a court of inquiry in the case of Major Granville O. Haller, late of the Seventh Infantry, United States Army.* 45th Congress, 2nd session, H.Res. 63.

US Congress, *Message from the President of the United States to the two houses of Congress at the commencement of the first session of the Thirty-four Congress.* 34th Congress, 1st session, 1855, House Ex. Doc. No. 1, Part 2, Serial 811.

US Senate, *The Committee on Military Affairs, to whom was referred the joint resolution (H.Res. 63) authorizing a court of inquiry in the case of Granville O. Haller, late of the Seventh Infantry, United States Army, having had the same under consideration, beg leave to submit the following report:*, 45th Congress, 3rd Session, Report No. 860.

United States War Department. *The War of the Rebellion: Official Records of the Union and Confederate Armies.* 70 vols. in 128 serials. Washington: Government Printing Office, 1880-1901.

INDEX

When a person's first name is not give it signifies that the first name is either unknown or not certain

A

Akerman, Amos, 121
Andrews, Col., 43, 44
Armistead, Maj., 41
Augur, Capt., 34

B

Bachman, John, 54
Baker, Supervisor of Indian Affairs, 45
Banks, Nathaniel, 52
Barnard, John, 48
Bates, Francis, 73, 74, 82
Beale, Mr., 46
Beaver, Col., 61
Belknap, Maj.William, 21
Belknap, William, 112
Belknap,William, 112
Bell, Robert, 19, 68
Bentz, Peter, 92, 108
Black, J.P., 14, 96
Bolan, Andrew, 28, 29, 32
Boyd, Capt., 58
Bradford, Gov., 95, 145
Brady, James, 59
Brady, P. R., 47
Brisbane, Col., 61
Brown, Mr., 42
Buchanan, James, 21
Buell, D. C., 41
Burgen, Henry, 54
Burnside, Ambrose, 9, 12, 82, 95, 150
Bush, Fred, 54

C

Cameron, Robert, 62
Ca-mi-a-kin. *See* Kamiarkin, Chief
Campbell, Mr., 38
Campion, W.H., 113
Carleton, James, 43
Casey, Silas, 36, 38, 48
Clarke, H.F., 77, 78, 79, 82, 86, 94, 104, 107, 117, 118

Colburn, A.V., 49, 51
Coppee, Henry, 58, 62
Couch, Darius, 12, 19, 50, 52, 53, 54, 58, 63, 87, 88, 90, 95
Covode, John, 80
Cox, Charlotte, 24
Cox, Ellen, 25, 26
Crane, Robert, 55, 64
Crocker, John, 74, 75, 85
Crooke, George, 62
Curry, George, 33, 34
Curtin, Gov. Andrew, 58, 62, 88, 89, 90
Cushing, Capt., 3, 5

D

Dallas, Mr., 37
Dana, Napoleon, 61
Davis, Jeff, 26, 138
Day, Lt., 31
Denny, John, 54
Devereux, J.H., 49
Dimmick, K. H., 42
Dryer, Mrs. (Capt.), 44
Du Barry, J.N., 62
Duck, Henry, 54
Dunn, Judge Advocate, 78, 106, 123

E

Evans, Barton, 63
Ewell, Richard, 60
Ewen, John, 62
Ewing, Charles, 78, 104, 132

F

Fasick, William, 54
Finney, S.W., 54
Franklin, E., 60
Franklin, William, 2, 3, 4, 6, 21, 96, 150
Frick, Jacob, 17, 53, 54, 58, 60, 63, 65, 66, 67, 68
Fried, George, 57
Fry, James, 95

G

Garland, John, 22, 94
Gibbs, George, 36
Gibson, Capt., 5
Gilbert, Gilbert, 54
Gracie, Lt., 29
Grant, Ulysses, 23, 112, 121, 122
Green, David, 55, 57, 65, 67, 68
Green, George, 54
Greene, O.D., 137

H

Haldeman, Charles, 57, 64, 67
Hall, Norman, 62
Halleck, Henry, 49, 53, 81, 103
Haller, George, 21
Haller, Granville, 1, 2, 3, 4, 5, 6, 7, 8, 9,
    11, 15, 16, 17, 18, 19, 21, 24, 25, 27,
    28, 31, 33, 38, 41, 42, 44, 47, 48, 49,
    50, 51, 52, 53, 54, 56, 59, 68, 69, 70,
    71, 72, 73, 74, 75, 76, 77, 78, 79, 80,
    81, 82, 83, 84, 85, 86, 87, 88, 89, 90,
    91, 92, 93, 94, 97, 98, 99, 100, 101,
    102, 103, 104, 105, 106, 107, 108,
    110, 111, 112, 115, 116, 117, 119,
    120, 122, 123, 124, 125, 126, 127,
    128, 129, 130, 131, 132, 133, 135,
    136, 137, 138, 139, 141, 143, 144,
    145, 146, 149, 150, 151
Haller, Henrietta, 25, 26
Haller, Susan, 21
Hamilton, John, 77, 78, 79, 82, 86, 94,
    104, 107
Hammond, George, 29
Hancock, Captain, 42, 59
Hardie, James, 110, 111, 112
Harney, William, 37, 38
Hatch, John, 50
Haupt, Herman, 9, 49, 50
Hayes, Rutherford, 112, 133
Hays, Jack, 42, 133
Haywood, Dr., 42
Henrietta Haller, 24
Henry, Lt. Col., 62
Henry, Patrick, 7, 143
Hersh, Edward, 149
Higgins, Col., 59
Holt, Joseph, 1, 81, 147, 148
Howard, Oliver, 135, 137
Hunt, George, 77, 78, 79, 82, 86, 94, 104, 107

I

Irwin, Commissary-General, 62
Ives, J. C., 46
Ives, Lt., 83

J

Jacobs, Orange, 19, 69
Jennings, Col., 19
Johnson, Albert, 73
Johnson, Andrew, 102, 121
Johnson, George, 47
Jones, Capt., 45, 61

K

Kamiarkin, Chief, 30, 32
Kelsey, Mr., 42
Kimmell, Francis, 62
Knipe, Joseph, 60, 61
Krause, William, 62

L

Lee, Robert E., 60, 61, 62, 90, 95
Legare, Hugh, 121, 131
Lewis, W.A.H., 62
Lincoln, Abraham, 4, 6, 97, 101, 102,
    103, 111, 116, 121, 125, 141, 150
Lockhard, John, 54
Luphart, Michael, 54

M

MacVeagh, Wayne, 62
Maish, Levi, 70, 71, 79, 89, 95, 108
Marcy, Mr., 37
Marcy, Randolph, 50, 52
Martin, Lt., 21, 45
McAllister, Charles, 62
McClellan, George, 1, 9, 47, 48, 49, 84,
    89, 95, 100, 115, 149, 150, 151
McClure, Col., 62
McConaughy, D., 20, 60
McConaughy, David, 62
McCrary, George, 119
McCreary, R. G., 17, 18
McDowell, Irvin, 51, 138
McGowan, Capt., 59
McLean Knox, Charles, 54, 64, 68

Mclerany, George, 135
Meade, George, 61
Meredith, William, 62
Miles, Col., 61
Miller, Jacob, 54
Milroy, Robert, 58, 59, 61, 90
Montgomery, Quartermaster, 25
Moore, A.P., 54
Mowry, Mr., 39
Mulholland, Sgt., 31
Murphy, Davis, 54
Murphy, Michael, 82

N

Neill, Thomas, 61
Nesmith, James, 33

O

Oliver, Joseph, 57

P

Peale, Wagon-master, 44
Petrikin, Reuben, 62
Pickett, George, 37, 38
Pierce, Col., 61
Platt, E.R., 139
Pleasonton, Alfred, 51
Poinsett, Joel, 21
Pope, Gen., 139
Porter, Andrew, 72, 95
Porter, Fitz-John, 96
Postley, G.A., 77, 78, 80, 82, 86, 94, 104, 107

R

Rains, Gabriel, 25, 26, 29, 31, 32, 33, 34
Randall, Lt., 64, 68
Raymond, Charles, 62
Rich, Jacob, 54
Ricketts, James, 96
Ridgway, Delaplaine, 64
Rigg, Edwin, 45, 46
Riley, Lt., 83
Roberts, Capt., 44
Robinson, Quartermaster, 140
Rollins, Maj., 42
Ross, Samuel, 103

Ruel, Issac, 54
Runkle, Benjamin, 112
Russell, A.L., 29, 62

S

Sanford, Mr., 43
Schenck, Robert, 52, 103, 104, 107, 145, 146
Scott, T.A., 62
Scott, Winfield, 23, 38
Sherman, William, 77, 137, 138
Shinck, James, 98
Showalter, Mr., 44
Shuman, Michael, 54
Sickles, William, 57, 68
Sigel, Franz, 61
Smith, E.K., 54
Smith, William, 59, 60, 61, 62
Spaulding, Lt., 3, 5
Spaulding, Mr., 3
Speed, James, 121
Spencer, George, 70
Stahel, Julius, 61
Stanton, Edwin, 8, 11, 58, 80, 97, 103, 146, 147
Stevens, Issac, 28, 31
Strickler, Capt., 57
Stumbaugh, Col., 62
Sumner, Edwin, 39, 42
Sweet, Sarah, 25

T

Taylor, Zachary, 22, 94
Thomas, Col., 60
Thomas, George, 102
Thomas, William, 66, 68
Thomas, William., 60
Thompson, Lt., 44
Tilton, James, 72
Townsend, E. D., 1, 77, 135, 137, 138
Tustenugge, Chief Halleck, 22

U

Up, Westly, 54

V

Vestal, Quartermaster, 44

W

Ward, Alexander, 25
Watts, Judge, 62
Wellman, Lt., 43
Wells, Clark, 1, 2, 3, 5, 6, 7, 8, 11, 12, 13, 14, 15, 16, 72, 73, 80, 81, 86, 89, 92, 93, 96, 97, 98, 99, 100, 101, 102, 115, 116, 117, 141, 143, 146, 147, 148, 149, 151
Wells, Gideon, 80
Welsh, Henry, 150
West, Col., 44
Wheeler, J.B., 59
Wheeling, Sgt., 44
Whiting, Charles, 1, 3, 4, 5, 6, 7, 8, 12, 13, 14, 16, 72, 98, 99, 116, 141, 143, 149, 150

Williams, George, 122
Williams, Seth, 51
Wills, David, 18
Wilson, Capt., 59
Wilson, Dr., 3
Wilson, Maj., 62
Wool, John, 26, 27, 28, 32, 35, 36
Worth, William, 22, 23
Wright, A., 62
Wright, George, 23, 34, 35, 37
Wright, John, 62

Y

Yates, Charles, 61, 62
Young, Samuel, 68

ABOUT THE AUTHOR

Guy Breshears received his BAE in Social Science Education from Eastern Washington University in Cheney, Washington. He participated in the Living American History Institute for Teachers program, 2001-2003. He resides in the state of Washington, where he has an interest in promoting the advancement of knowledge, understanding and preservation of the military events that took place while it was a Territory, in part by maintaining a website called WashingtonWars.net. He is a member of the Pacific Northwest Historian's Guild and the Kennesaw Mountain Historical Association. His first book, *Loyal till Death: A Diary of the 13th New York Artillery,* was published in 2003 by Heritage Books.

www.ingramcontent.com/pod-product-compliance
Lightning Source LLC
Chambersburg PA
CBHW071428160426
43195CB00013B/1847